THE SPIRIT OF THE
LEGAL PROFESSION

LONDON · HUMPHREY MILFORD
OXFORD UNIVERSITY PRESS

THE SPIRIT OF THE LEGAL PROFESSION

BY

ROBERT N. WILKIN

THE MORE EXTENSIVE A MAN'S KNOWLEDGE
OF WHAT HAS BEEN DONE
THE GREATER WILL BE HIS POWER
OF KNOWING WHAT TO DO

DISRAELI

1938

PUBLISHED FOR THE COLLEGE OF LAW
OF THE OHIO STATE UNIVERSITY BY
YALE UNIVERSITY PRESS NEW HAVEN

FOREWORD

THIS little book contains the substance of addresses delivered to the student body of The Ohio State University College of Law and represents views that have matured and crystallized in the mind of an outstanding lawyer, after three decades of professional experience and several years of work as a member of the Committees on Judicial Administration and Legal Reform of the Ohio State Bar Association and Judicial Selection of the American Bar Association. Its purpose is to show that, during the years, whenever the professional influence has predominated there have been good judges and efficient administration of justice, and that the contrary has been true whenever that influence has been subordinated to imperial, political, or commercial influences. A thoughtful retracing of "the struggle for law" was necessary, though Judge Wilkin makes no claim to original research. Established facts have been considered and an attempt made by their interpretation to show forth the spirit of the legal profession.

When the profession as a whole is damned because of its relatively few derelicts, it is indeed timely that attention be called to its truly heroic services and noteworthy accomplishments. Shakespeare makes Mark Antony say, in his famous oration in *Julius Caesar:*

"The evil that men do lives after them,
The good is oft interred with their bones."

Some may question the universal accuracy of this generalization, but it cannot be denied that there is truth in it, to the extent that evil conduct is discussed to the exclusion of the good.

American lawyers should be grateful to Judge Wilkin for sounding a true note in the general chorus of undiscriminating derogation of the legal profession.

HERSCHEL W. ARANT.

The Ohio State University,
July, 1938.

CONTENTS

viii CONTENTS

PART 3: IN AMERICA

PART 4: IN RETROSPECT AND PROSPECT

PART ONE

THE SPIRIT OF THE LEGAL PROFESSION

IN ROME

THE SPIRIT OF THE
LEGAL PROFESSION

I.

THE GIFT OF THE LAW

THE law is the gift of Rome to the world. By the word *law* is meant the body or system of rules for man's civil conduct which is enforced in courts of justice. As used here it means something more general than civil or municipal law and something not so general or vague as international or natural law. Using it in this sense we may say that the law of every civilized country is an extension or development of, or has been greatly influenced by, the law as conceived during the Roman Republic and developed during the Roman Empire.

Prior to the time of the Roman Republic there were laws, but no such concept as the law. There were tribal and customary rules, imperial edicts, and religious commandments. There were the Code of Hammurabi, the Ten Commandments, the Torah. Such laws were usually shrouded in mystery and religious superstition. They were for the most part arbitrary and inflexible, like the proverbial laws of the Medes and Persians. There were decrees and enactments of judicial and legislative assemblies. But each was usually made for a specific need, and they lacked relation and unity. But when the Romans were called upon to administer the laws of different countries they began to study the principles that were common to all. Roman necessity and Roman genius conspired to give us the science of law. Plato had written his dialogue on the laws—a very discursive treatment. But it remained for the Romans to give us jurisprudence. Its Roman origin is indicated by its Latin name. If it had been developed earlier no doubt like most other sciences and philosophies it would have had a Greek name.

The law is certainly one of man's greatest achievements. It indicates the extent of his evolution. The law of the state, or we might say the state of the law, is a true criterion of a nation's civilization. If we think of a moral order of the universe, of which man is given some premonition through his conscience and toward which he is moved by his aspiration for justice, we may say that the law is his closest approximation to universal harmony. It represents his finest practical efforts to realize his social ideal.

As it comes to us today it has of course been modified and improved by the contributions of other nations, ages, and agencies. It has been profoundly affected by the canon law and the influence of the church generally. It has been expanded by the customs of trade and the law merchant. England has contributed notably to its administration through the development of the jury and an independent judiciary. But still we can truthfully say that the law came to the world through Rome, just as we say that philosophy and art came through Greece.

To be more specific and more accurate, however, we should say that the law has been brought to the world by the spirit of the legal profession. While it has come to us mainly through Roman institutions, it is the work of men who in many instances were not Romans. The part of it which was most Roman was contributed to by men from the provinces and other countries. During the Republic many of the leading jurists were provincials and during the Empire, to mention

but a few of the legal lights, Quintilian came
from Spain, Papinian and Ulpian from Syria,
and Salvius Julianus from Africa. The Greek
influence was always great, and of course the
great Justinian Digest was compiled and
published at Constantinople. As indicated it
was the international or cosmopolitan nature
of the Roman government that stimulated
the development of the law. The spirit of the
profession has never been entirely national-
ized or temporized.

By spirit of the profession is meant that
animus, that afflatus, that inspiration which
has moved so many great men to love, to
study, to teach, to practice, and to establish
the law. Spirit of the profession is used rather
than profession because the profession has always contained some second-rate fellows who
have reduced their vocation to a trade; who
from earliest times have been referred to as
trimmers, barkers, hawkers, shysters, and
mountebanks; who have memorized the laws,
practiced the tricks of the trade, and bartered
their talents to any cause that would pay a
price. Selfish gain has been their only motive.
But in striking contrast to them are the men

who have been moved by the professional spirit—men whose performance has followed their profession. Theirs is a record of unselfish devotion, moral courage, and fine accomplishment—a record of which the world, if it were truly informed, could be justly proud.

II.

BIRTH OF THE PROFESSION

THE establishment of the law and the formation of the legal profession were coincident and contemporaneous. As men devoted themselves to the study of legal principles, the law was produced, and this in turn brought forth a body of men who made it their calling. In the early Republic the old customary law, both sacred and secular, was in the control of the priests, pontiffs. Their civil responsibilities had come to them originally as counselors of the kings. Even after the posting of the Twelve Tables in the Forum, the pontiffs still controlled the interpretation and much of the administration of the law. Through their regulation of the calendar they determined on what days actions could be started, through their formation of the writs of action they influenced the course of litigation, and through their opinions (*responsa*) they determined how the law should be applied. But such an esoteric confinement of legal knowledge could not be expected to satisfy a self-governing people. As Romans took more part in government there was a growth of feeling that the law should be made more available.

When therefore Appius Claudius had facilitated trade and the use of water by the construction of the first aqueduct and the great Roman road (*Via Appia*), he next authorized his legal clerk, Gnaeus Flavius, to make the law more accessible by publishing the forms of legal actions (*legis actiones*) and the calendar, so that Romans might know how and when their cases could be filed and heard. His was one of the earliest works on the law (*Ius Civile Flavianum*, 304 B.C.).

In a representative republic like Rome, with its annual elections, outstanding men were continually being trained in public office and legal affairs. And these were appealed to more and more for advice and counsel by

their less experienced neighbors. Such of
these public men as were blessed with facility
of speech were also requested to be spokesmen at public trials for the less voluble and
more timid citizens. Thus sprang up a body
of men who acted as attorneys and counselors at law. In their personal relation to clients they supplanted the ancient *patroni*, and
at first rivaled and finally superseded the
pontiffs in the direction of legal affairs.

These lawyers developed a justifiable
pride, a professional feeling, *esprit de corps*,
in the position they occupied. To be appealed
to for help, to be asked to champion others,
to be placed in a position of public confidence
challenged their character and stimulated
their sense of loyalty and desire to serve.
Their study of the law expanded their idea
of the purpose of the law. From their com-
prehension of the interrelation of laws they
were led to the conception of a system of
law. The *Commentaria Tripertita*, "the
cradle of juristic literature," was published
(Sextus Catus, 194 B.C.), containing the
Twelve Tables with commentary, the inter-
pretations of the jurists, and forms of proce-

dure. Scaevola (President of the Senate and Cicero's tutor) wrote a treatise which for the first time analyzed and classified the law according to subjects treated (95 B.C.).

From the establishment of the Republic the principal judicial functions had devolved on the praetor. He, like the other chief magistrates, was elected by the people—voting in groups it should be noted, in *comitia centuriata*, not in *comitia curiata* or by plebiscite. Frequently the men elevated to this office were not versed in the law; and while at first they had depended on the *responsa* or opinions of the pontiffs, they came in time to use with increasing frequency the opinions of the lawyers who were recognized for their learning and experience. Thus grew up a class of specialists, the jurisconsults, who acted as advisers or counsel to the most active practitioners and to clients and magistrates. In the beginning their service was voluntary and unofficial but under Augustus certain eminent jurisconsults were granted the right (*ius respondendi*) to give opinions which, in absence of conflicting opinion, the magistrates were bound to follow. These opinions were in writing and carefully considered. Because the Romans gave the function of the jurisconsults important place, the opinions of these great jurists naturally influenced the course of legal development and came in time to embody much of the Roman law.

As the Roman legions expanded their country's dominion into a world empire, the proconsuls and procurators followed the military commanders into the conquered provinces to establish the law and maintain civil order. It became a custom for these provincial governors to publish edicts which set out the general principles of law by which the province was to be ruled. Mucius Scaevola, mentioned above, prepared one of the earliest of such edicts for the direction of legal affairs in Asia. Cicero later made it the model of his edict when he became proconsul for Cilicia, and his administration became famous for its fairness. So other governors copied the edicts of the great lawyers or called other lawyers into the preparation of new edicts, and thus the work of the Roman jurists was extended and expanded.

These provincial governors found it a very

wise practice to adopt and maintain as much of the local legal arrangement as was consistent with Roman colonial policy. The wise and humane administrators prided themselves upon the amount of local autonomy allowed their subjects. The Roman system was thus affected to some extent by the local laws which it supplanted. This foreign influence was, moreover, not confined to the provinces. Rome became the business metropolis as well as the civil capital of the world. Not only all roads but also all shipping lanes led to Rome. They all merged into the *Via Sacra* of the Roman Forum. The city acquired a great foreign population and a world-wide trade. It became necessary for Rome itself to take account of the laws which its foreign populace knew and which had guided so many businessmen in their important transactions. So great was the legal business of this nature that a special judicial officer, *praetor peregrinus*, was provided to hear cases in which non-Romans were involved.

With so general an expansion of life, it is no wonder that Rome began to feel legal growing-pains. The Twelve Tables and the

formularies of the pontiffs began to pinch—
they could not themselves stretch to fit the
needs of the new life. The *Lex Aebutia* was
therefore passed which, while strictly a pro-
cedural statute, permitted the development
of general equitable jurisdiction and a body
of praetorian law. Under the influence of this
development it became the practice of the
chief judicial officer, the *praetor urbanus*, at
the beginning of his term to set up an edict
stating his general principles for interpretation of the laws, suggesting relief from old
legal severities, legalizing, in fact, evasions
of the strict letter of the law, introducing
methods to simplify procedure, and in general allowing for the changes made necessary
by the changing times. Since the praetor was
frequently not a jurist himself he sought the
assistance of some lawyer who had the special knowledge required to draft the new
clauses of the edict, the old clauses being
copied from earlier edicts. These edicts became in time the embodiment of a very
important part of the Roman law and a principal source of instruction for future students.
Thus another great branch of Roman juris-

prudence was developed under the influence of, and in turn influenced, the spirit of the profession.

III.

GROWTH OF THE PROFESSION

IT is remarkable that the professional influence survived the Republic. In spite of the general disintegration of republican institutions, the weakness of the Senate, the growth of mob violence, the corruption of juries, the perjury of witnesses, the changeableness of law officers, the tyranny of dictators—in spite of all these, the Roman legal system survived and continued under the Empire. This was true because there was a spirit of the legal profession which held itself above and beyond the ruck and reel of worldly affairs.

The establishment of the Empire no doubt arrested the general corruption of society and stabilized government so that the legal system could survive. We need not, however, deal in detail with its history under the Empire. Republican legal history is more important because it records the inception of the ideas and institutions which were the basis of all future development. The so-called classical period of Roman law was not creative. What remained for the jurists of the Empire was to elaborate, refine, and digest.

The important point is that the inception, the development, and the refinement of the world's legal system were all under the direct and continuous influence of those great men who were imbued with the spirit of the law. This fact has been recognized generally by historians. Professor Theodore W. Dwight, discussing the general equitable jurisdiction of the praetor in his introduction to Maine's *Ancient Law*, says:

It might seem at first thought that there was no limit by which this extensive power was confined, and that the action of the praetor might become dangerous to social order. Practically, his power was restrained by the ideas and views of the legal profession to which he belonged.

Professor Frank Gardner Moore, in his recent work on *The Roman's World*, in discussing the same subject, says:

It was by this means that the inflexibility of statutory law—the Twelve Tables and subsequent legislation—was made to yield to the demands of equity. Legislation to modernize obsolete provisions became unnecessary when the same object could be accomplished by a few words added to the praetor's white-board (*album*) set up near his tribunal in the Forum. With expert opinion behind him the praetor was in small danger of going too far.

And continuing his observation down to a later period:

Even the most tyrannical emperors seldom interfered with the development or the practice of private law, in spite of the fact that the leaders in jurisprudence were almost exclusively senators and in their philosophy Stoics, hence inclined to side with the opposition.

And Professor F. de Zulueta points out how the work of the lawyer, the draft of some bold pleader, and the manipulation of the formulary system would make its way into the edict. He says that the edict, "though formally the magistrates' contribution to practice, was substantially the work of the jurists." And then he observes that the work of that profession, jurisprudence, is always present and contains within itself the precipitate of all other factors.

IV.

PROFESSION NOT A TRADE

It is not to be inferred from the word *profession* that the lawyers of early times were organized into a body like the modern bar association. They did not think of themselves as a guild or of their work as a trade. They had not that much class consciousness or selfish interest. They had no legal recognition as a profession until after the Empire was established. There were no specified requirements for admission, no license to practice. There were no law schools; only law teachers. The basis of membership was confidence—one had to have enough character and ability to beget and keep self-confidence and the confidence of others.

But there was a professional feeling, born of common ideals, purposes, and practices. The first evidence of such feeling—and always a mark of true professional feeling—was the willingness of older members to assist the younger. Scaevola taught Cicero, who in turn taught Caesar and Brutus and became the model for Quintilian and succeeding generations. Quintilian taught Pliny. Labeo and

Capito, "the two ornaments of peace," studied the writings of the republican era and then taught the youths of the reign of Augustus and of Tiberius. The writings of the earlier masters were continually studied by those who followed in their footsteps, and the accomplishment of one generation became the inspiration of the next. The spirit of the profession prompted each age to succeed, and if possible to exceed, its predecessor.

These early lawyers, while more than professional clansmen, were also more than legal technicians. The word-jugglers and hidebound logicians were to them objects of contempt. Cicero voiced his disgust for the tricksters and barkers and Quintilian deplored the "acrobats in eloquence," who, he said, "do not study, understand men, read hearts, appeal to right or eternal justice." In his work on advocacy he said the great lawyer should not only study the edicts of the praetors and the opinions of the jurists, but should also reflect on the nature of happiness, the foundation of morality, and on all that pertains to the good and the true. He thought the lawyer should be accomplished like Cicero and good like Cato. This idea of the profes-

sion finally found a place at the very beginning of the Digest: "Jurisprudence is the
study of the good and the just."

The professional pioneers displayed the
very widest intellectual interest. They might
have been classified generally as advocates
(orators), counselors, writers, and administrators; but the work of hardly any would
fall wholly within one classification. Scaevola, as stated, was writer and administrator;
Cicero was advocate, administrator, and
writer; his friend Sulpicius was counselor,
administrator, and writer; Quintilian and
Pliny were advocates and writers. Their interest moreover ranged far beyond the law.
Most of them had had experience as military
commanders, some as naval commanders—
Pliny the Elder being in command of the
fleet when he lost his life at the time of the
great eruption of Vesuvius. The subjects they
studied and wrote about ranged from philosophy to agriculture, from poetry to finance.
Many were historians of high rank; and they
were so observing and intelligent that even
their casual and personal letters, like those of
Cicero and Pliny, are now original sources of
the greatest historic value.

But in all their interests the predominant Roman trait is apparent; all knowledge is brought to bear upon their understanding of the law of man's nature. Even their greatest attempts in natural science, like those of Pliny the Elder and Seneca, were turned to ethical account. They may not rate as the world's greatest philosophers, but they crystallized much of Greek philosophy into Roman law. That all men are equal before the law was a legal rule in Rome; in Greece it had been a philosophical concept; in modern times it became a political dogma. The Roman lawyers, in this instance as in many others, gave the idea its greatest practical value, if not its only value. They brought all knowledge to the service of the law and made the practice of the law a service in statesmanship.

That the great Roman lawyers maintained standards of unselfish conduct may be inferred from the fact that in their philosophy they were Stoics. We have moreover very specific proof of high professional standards. One clear instance of such proof is a letter which Cicero wrote to Trebatius. We know that Trebatius was also a lawyer because

Cicero once wrote of him to Caesar: "As to his character, I pledge myself for this . . . that a truer-hearted man, and a braver and less assuming man, does not exist: add to this that he is quite at the top of his profession in civil law because of his unequalled memory and vast learning." To Trebatius, Cicero wrote:

I was wondering at the long intermission of your letters, when my friend Pansa accounted for your indifference by assuring me that you were turned an Epicurean. I have been in some pain for your principles, I confess, ever since your intimacy with my friend Seius. But how will you reconcile your tenets to your profession, and act for the interest of your client, now that you have adopted the maxim of doing nothing but for your own? With what grace can you insert the usual clause in your deeds of agreement: "The parties to these presents, as becomes good men and true." For neither truth nor trust can there be in those who professedly govern themselves upon motive of absolute selfishness. I am in some pain, likewise, how you will settle the law concerning the partition of "rights in common": as there can be nothing in common between those who make their own private gratification the sole criterion of right and wrong. Or can you think it proper to administer an oath, while you maintain that Jupiter is incapable of all resent-

ment? In a word, what will become of the good
people of Ulubrae who have placed themselves under your protection, if you hold the maxim of your
sect, "that a wise man ought not to engage himself
in public affairs"? In good earnest I shall be ex-
tremely sorry if it is true that you have really de-
serted us. But if your conversion is nothing more
than a convenient compliment to the opinions of
Pansa, I will forgive your dissimulation, provided
you let me know soon how your affairs go on, and
in what manner I can be of any service in them.
Farewell.

Just a bit of pleasantry between friends,
half serious, half bantering! Yet it clearly
reveals to us that the lawyers of the Roman
republic imposed upon themselves very definite obligations to one another, to their clients, and to the public.

V.

MASTERS OF THE WORD

THESE founders of the profession were masters of the word, both spoken and written.
They are more generally thought of as orators, but their greatest skill was in writing.
There was less affectation, less occasion for
stage play, in their writing than in their

speaking. Cicero's writings are so definitely a part of general classical literature that we do not think of him as a legal writer—nor was he, in the strict sense. But he was always devoted to the law—a champion of its aims, justice and order. To that end, and because he hated the arbitrary rule of dictators, he literally and figuratively gave his hand and his head to the Republic—and lost all. But his writings, especially his *De Republica* and *De Officiis*, have been a source of inspiration to the founders of future republics. Therein may be found the exposition of that balance of elements of government which eventually crystallized in the American Constitution. Another eminent writer of the same period, who confined his efforts more strictly to the law, was Cicero's friend Servius Sulpicius. His work has survived only in quotations in the Digest, but we know his influence was great in the early Empire. We know also that he was a master of literary expression, not only because Cicero said so, but because the letter of condolence which he wrote when Cicero's daughter Tullia died has been preserved.

As the science of law developed, the writing of lawyers was confined more strictly to the law. But in its classical period jurisprudence assumed a virtue and brilliance beyond all other forms of literature or intellectual endeavor. The original writings of the masters of that period, Papinian, Ulpian, Paulus, Modestinus, are almost entirely lost, but the extensive quotations in the Digest are proof of their merit. One of the works of Gaius, however, and the model for Justinian's *Institutes*, has come to us almost intact. It is a handbook for beginners and is a model of Latin style. It illustrates the general taste and standards of those times and may well serve as model for our times; it is straightforward and elevated, clear, terse, and unaffected. Since the lawyer is the oracle of the law he should be able to speak of it with logical power and write it in the plainest terms.

VI.

THE VOICE OF A NEED

Not only is the lawyer the oracle of the law, he is the voice of one of humanity's deep and abiding needs. The profession was not carved out of whole cloth for its own purposes; it came into existence, and continues to exist, in answer to one of the primitive cravings of the human heart. Early in history man expressed his yearning for a champion to meet his accusers at the gate. Since to err is human, a defender is a human need. In the hurly-burly of life, moreover, with all its crosscurrents of human interest, misunderstandings seem inevitable, and when men disagree they have need of spokesmen for their respective causes. Feelings grow tense and negotiations would be impossible except through intermediaries. When man is most vitally affected, he has greatest need of disinterested counsel. At such times things need to be said which cannot be said to advantage by oneself. In the end if wrongs cannot be righted and differences dissolved by the parties themselves, not only they, but society at large, have need of an arbiter to preserve the peace.

It is proof of man's charity to man that he has provided that when man stands accused he shall not stand alone. To be accused is to be in part condemned. To stand charged with crime in the public forum, to be indicted be-

fore the bar of justice, leaves one speechless.
To speak in one's own behalf defeats one's
purpose. Self-praise makes one a braggart.
To be arrogant and voluble gives credit to
one's accusers. One's weakness is one's only
strength. But, thanks to the legal profession,
that weakness has not been left defenseless.
Cicero defied the hired accuser of the ruthless
dictator Sulla in order to champion the cause
of Roscius. Doubting his own ability to do
well what older men had feared to under-
take, he comforted himself with the thought
that he would do the best he could and that
"at least Roscius would not find himself
without counsel." Malesherbes defied the
revolutionary mob—more terrible than a dictator because more senseless—in order to defend his former sovereign, Louis XVI.
Though no longer a monarch Louis was still
a man, and his counsel therefore stood for
him at the bar—and followed him to the
guillotine. Hale defied Cromwell and Erskine
defied the very judge on the bench in order to
defend the sacred right and duty of a lawyer
to act for his client. Finally this right and
duty, championed by many lawyers through
many years, received sanction in the charter

of the American republic. The magnanimity of the law is preserved even against its offenders. Man may be accused but not abandoned, foresworn but not forsaken. This constitutional guaranty of the right of counsel is the gift to humanity of the spirit of the profession.

PART TWO

THE SPIRIT OF THE
LEGAL PROFESSION

IN ENGLAND

VII.

GIFT OF THE COMMON LAW

HAVING outlined the professional influence in the development of the principal legal system of the world, it would be possible to show that the same influence was an important factor in the development of every other system of law. It would not be possible—nor is it the purpose of this essay—to show that the great lawyers were the sole source of the law. They no doubt, like the law, were the product of deeper influences, racial, social, economic; but still they were the principal instruments through which those forces worked. As Dean Pound has said in *The Spirit of the Common Law:*

Undoubtedly the great lawyer has not been the least factor in legal history. Roman law without Papinian and Ulpian and Paul, the civil law of the modern world without Bartolus, international law without Grotius, French law without Pothier, German law without Savigny, the common law without Coke, or American constitutional law without Marshall, are almost unthinkable.

While it is not necessary to trace the professional influence through the development of each system of law, still a treatment of the subject would be incomplete if it did not consider that influence with reference to the especial gift of the second greatest legal system of the world—the independent judiciary of the common law.

Before there could be an independent judiciary there had to be a separation of the judicial function from other activities of government. In Roman jurisprudence such differentiation was not planned. There was of course some separation as matter of practice. The very volume of legal business required almost the entire attention of the praetors, and other duties were therefore almost excluded. But the functions of each of the principal Roman officers extended into all fields of government—legislative, executive, and judicial. The consuls, though the chief executives, presided over the Senate, over assemblies of the people, and at certain trials. The praetors, next in rank, though engaged for the most part in the direction of litigation, took part also in legislation and could on occasion command armies and assist the consuls in other executive duties. The aediles, who were in charge of public works, buildings, and games, had also superintendence of the police, with power to hear complaints of crimes and to impose punishment. The Senate itself, although originally a council, later absorbed a great part of the executive and judicial functions. The Romans talked about *potestas*, or general creative power, *imperium*, sovereign executive or military authority, and *jurisdictio*, or purely legal authority; but they did not divide the functions of the different public offices along those lines.

Montesquieu is generally referred to as the prime expositor of the three great divisions of government because his work on *The Spirit of Laws* was popular at the time of the formation of the American republic. He was read and quoted so extensively that he came to be thought of as the originator of the balance of powers, in spite of the fact that the *Federalist* and he himself pointed out that the English Constitution was his model. The first three divisions of our Constitution are still referred to as "The Montesquieu separation of threefold powers." But the truth is, such separation was well developed in England when he first visited that country before he wrote his book.

The divorcement of the judicial function from entangling alliance with other political duties had its origin in that doctrine which is generally referred to as "the supremacy of law." That doctrine holds that all agencies of government are bound to act upon principle and reason, and may not follow arbitrary will or mere caprice. It is the base of that legal development which has given us not only the distinction of the judicial function from other functions of government, but trial by jury, the influence of judicial precedent, the principle of due process, and finally an independent judiciary. That doctrine is the foundation of Magna Charta, the Bill of Rights, the Constitution, and all our liberties.

Historically, as Dean Pound says, it goes back to a fundamental notion of Germanic law, a belief in a law founded upon eternal intrinsic reasonableness which is above and beyond mere will. It led to the conviction that those who wield authority should be held to such acts as conform to that law. The doctrine received its full development in England, because in Germany it came into too close contact with the Roman conception that the will of the sovereign had the force of law. Montesquieu says:

In perusing the admirable treatise of Tacitus "On the Manners of the Germans," we find it is from that nation the English have borrowed the idea of their political government. This beautiful system was invented first in the woods.

Certain it is that in earliest times, under the Saxon kings, Englishmen had their local courts for the redress of grievances, together with the well-established custom of referring disputes over facts to a jury from the neighborhood. As the absurdity and cruelty of the ordeal and trial by battle, with their appeal to superstition and force, had become apparent, men entrusted the settlement of their disputes to their peers, with an appeal to their inherent reasonableness and sense of fairness. This practice was so well established by the year 1066 that even the Norman conquerors had to accept it. For some time after the Conquest few causes were carried before the royal tribunals, Englishmen finding readier courts of justice in the manors or counties to which they belonged. On account of this attachment to local courts Henry II established itinerant justices to decide civil and criminal pleas within each county. He was prompted to do so no doubt by two considerations: resort by Englishmen to courts presided over by judges of his appointment would tend to increase (1) his authority and (2) his revenue.

As the jurisdiction of these royal justices became more familiar, and as it seemed less liable to partiality or intimidation than the provincial courts, suitors grew willing to submit to it, and it was eventually confirmed in Magna Charta by an express provision for an annual visitation. That great charter also provided that no freeman should be taken or imprisoned, or disseized of his lands or his liberties, or exiled, or destroyed, or passed upon, or sent upon, "but by lawful judgment of his peers, or by the law of the land." Therein King John was compelled to promise: "We will sell to no man, we will not deny or delay to any man, justice or right." And then a detached administration of justice was ordained by the provision that the court of common pleas should not follow the crown "but be held in some certain place." Thus was instituted the great common pleas bench of Westminster with full and exclusive jurisdiction over all private civil disputes. But it should always be remembered that Magna Charta did not grant or create these rights. It was merely the instrument by which the king was forced to acknowledge them. They were born of an instinct for justice and the spirit of the common law.

VIII.

BIRTH OF THE ENGLISH BAR

IT is to the establishment of the king's court that we owe the uniformity of our common law, and the development of the legal profession. Without its supervisory jurisdiction the common law would have remained only a mass of local customs administered by laymen. The earliest publication of the common law, Glanvil's treatise, is held to contain the rules followed by the Norman officers of the king's court in interpreting and applying that law. The fundamentals of our legal system were set down during the last of the reign of Henry III when the customs of the

common law and the forms and the precedents of the courts were analyzed and di-
gested into the great work of Bracton. The
work of that great lawyer and judge became
the cornerstone of the common law and the
security of public freedom. Thereafter the
capacity of deciding legal controversies was
to be found only in men who had devoted
themselves to that peculiar study.

Magna Charta proved to be not so much a
treaty of peace as a declaration of war. King
John acknowledged it but immediately proceeded to violate it. Though its acknowledgment was prompt, its acceptance was pro-
longed. It was not adopted into the English
Constitution, it was worked into it. It was not
established until its acknowledgment by succeeding sovereigns had been repeatedly enforced. Its principles were made a part of the
basic law of the land through the patient devotion, zealous adherence, intellectual integrity, and heroic courage of those men who
professed the law. The rugged idea which
Montesquieu says was first discovered in the
Germanic tribes was finally developed into a
beautiful system under the aegis of the legal
profession.

There was a more definite organization of the profession in England than there had been in Rome. This was brought about by many causes, the chief of which was the segregation of the law courts, as has been mentioned. The localizing of the practice served to integrate the profession. The general interest in the law had led naturally to the study of the law. We know that during the twelfth and thirteenth centuries there were schools of law in London under the control of the clergy. These were abolished by a decree of Henry III prohibiting the holding of such schools in the city and by a papal bull forbidding the clergy to teach the common law. The pope and the king no doubt attributed the independence of the bishops and barons of England to too great a familiarity with the vigorous spirit of that law. The bishops and barons had based their opposition to the king's levies and prerogative on that law. For instance, when the pope ordered the clergy to raise money to pay for the Sicilian crown which he had offered to the king's son, the Bishop of London had said, "The Pope and the King together may take the mitre off my head; but, if they do, they will find that I shall put on a soldier's helmet. I pay nothing." Other bishops and many barons followed his example.

But the profession was not suppressed by king's decree or papal bull. Banished from the city, its members assembled in a suburb beyond the wall. Denied the benefit of clergy as teachers, the profession raised up its own instructors. The enforcement of the provisions of Magna Charta had led by this time to the firm establishment of the Court of Common Pleas at Westminster Hall. As a result the judges and practitioners of the law had begun to gather in that neighborhood. When the city law schools were turned adrift they found new lodgment at Holborn, a village in the open country east of London and adjacent to Westminster. The judges, professors, and students lived together in the inns and hostelries of the neighborhood. In time the lawyers began to organize into groups, like the guilds of that period, and took over some of the principal houses of the vicinity for their abodes. In the neighborhood were the manor houses of the Earl of Lincoln and of the Baron Grey de Wilton, which became Lincoln's Inn and Gray's Inn, and the churches and quarters of the Knights Templars were leased by two other legal societies which came to be known as Middle Temple and Inner Temple. These four great Inns of Court constituted thereafter the home of the legal fraternity. Fortescue described them as an academy for those who apply themselves to the study of the law; and Blackstone referred to them as "Our Judicial University."

The principal way between these Inns of Court was a lane which ran from Holborn down to the river. It was flanked on the east by the estate of the Bishop of Chichester, which afterwards became a part of Lincoln's Inn. When Ralph Neville was Bishop of Chichester he was also Lord High Chancellor and the lane was called Chancellor's Lane. This name became abbreviated into Chancery Lane. The lane itself became exalted into the *Via Sacra* of English jurisprudence.

Fortescue gives an account of the schooling which the young men received from the Inns of Court. He said they learned singing and all kinds of music, dancing, and such other accomplishments and diversions as were suitable to their quality. Upon festival days, after the offices of the church were

over, they employed themselves in the study
of sacred and profane history. He said that
everything which was good and virtuous was
to be learned and all vice discouraged and
banished. The youth of the nobility attended
"not so much to make the laws their study,
much less to live by the profession, having
large patrimonies of their own, but to form
their manners and to preserve them from the
contagion of vice." It became a part of the
education of a gentleman to understand the
laws of his land. Fortescue said the discipline
was excellent and that there was harmony
between the Inns and friendship among the
members. A high standard of scholarship was
maintained.

So general was the training, indeed, that
the Inns became a source of English letters
as well as of English law. No literary history
of England can overlook the influence of the
Inns of Court. Many of its masters had been
students there. Inner Temple claims Chau-
cer, Beaumont, Hallam, Boswell; Middle
Temple, Cowper, Moore, Dickens, Thackeray, Goldsmith, Lamb, Dr. Johnson, and
Thomas de Quincy; Gray's Inn, Sir Francis
Bacon and Sir Philip Sidney; and Lincoln's

Inn, Sir Thomas More, T. B. Macaulay, and
Edward Bulwer-Lytton. And this list is illus-
trative rather than exhaustive. Many literary
lights, like Thackeray and Macaulay, had
been barristers as well as students. Some no
doubt, like Dickens and Thackeray, were in-
debted to the Inns for the facility with which
they made their legal characterizations.
Though they left the law, their influence returned upon the law. Their literary portrayal
of evils had a profound reaction upon legal
procedure.

It was largely through the Inns of Court
that the spirit of the legal profession was impressed upon the governing class of England
and the general literature of English-speaking people. It was due to the breadth and
comprehensiveness of the professional influence that English law was so effective in
molding social and political development.
Early in its history the legal profession took
on somewhat of the catholicity of the bishops
and barons so influential in its founding. The
Holy Fathers of the Church, in spite of their
strict doctrine of one faith and one church,
had never entirely excluded all who were ex-
teriorly of other communions, but held that

those who seek the truth with anxious solici-
tude, "in virtue of the disposition of their
hearts, belong to the Catholic Church." So
the legal profession has always accepted into
its communion all those who are moved by
its spirit to seek and serve the law.

But while the Inns of Court were broad in
their influence, they were strict in their training. Fortescue said: "The manner and method
how the laws are professed and studied in
those places, is pleasant and excellently well
adapted for proficiency." The instructors
were called "Readers," and many of their
"Readings," or lectures, were long remembered in the profession for their learning and
excellence. For example, Littleton's work on
Tenures, Coke's on Fines, Bacon's on Uses,
and Dyer's on Wills, were all originally
"Readings." Of course the classics of English
legal literature, such as Coke's Commentaries
and Blackstone's Commentaries, as well as
such writings as those of Jeremy Bentham
and John Austin, had their inspiration in the
Inns of Court. Nearly all the great barristers
and judges of England were trained as lawyers by the Inns, and they in turn had their
influence upon the instruction of succeeding

students. It was judicially determined by Lord Mansfield that, while the courts had no jurisdiction over the Inns "according to the general law of the land"; yet "in every instance their conduct is subject to the control of the Judges as visitors."

The holding of "Moots" was a part of the course of instruction. These consisted of arguments of cases propounded by the "Put Case" and were presided over by a "Reader" or "Bencher." They afforded practice in a kind of mimic lawsuit. The conduct of these "Moots" must have been quite realistic because of the usual presence of members of the bench and the bar. While there was a marked differentiation of classes and grades, yet there was a constant association of all members of the profession. Judges and barristers lived at the Inns and students attended the sessions of the near-by courts. While the professional influence was liberally spread abroad, it was kept intense at home. The world has never known a greater concentration of professional tradition and influence than that of the Inns of Court. Ben Jonson called them "the noblest nurseries of humanity and liberty in the Kingdom." For nearly six hundred years they have been a pure and unfailing fount of legal inspiration.

It was natural, after the lawyers had supplanted the clergy as teachers, that they should soon supplant them as judges. As the profession completed its natural development it began to supply the men necessary for all professional posts. In the earlier days of England, as elsewhere in Europe, the ecclesiastics, being the educated men, did most of the technical legal work. They issued the writs and kept what legal records were kept. The Norman conquerors at first depended upon them almost exclusively for judges of the king's courts. But soon after Magna Charta, we begin to read, as Maitland says, of men climbing from the bar to the bench. At first the influence of the clergy was removed from the county courts, and the jurisdiction of the bishops was restricted to the settlement of estates and domestic relations. The lay lawyers and judges were quite jealous of their acquired authority and it was not long until they were issuing writs of prohibition against encroachments upon their jurisdiction. In spite of the resistance of the churchmen, the church was finally excluded from the exer-

cise of temporal power, and lawyers trained
by the profession became the judges of all
the courts.

IX.

THE KING AND THE
JUDICIARY

ALTHOUGH the law courts were no longer an
appanage of the king's person, the judges of
the courts were for a long time subject to the
king's influence. The courts had become separate instruments for the administration of
public justice, but the judges were still appointed by the king. The kings therefore
through successive reigns adhered tenaciously
to the view that the judges were their ministers and that the function of the judges was
subordinate to the royal prerogative. The independence of the judiciary was not secured
until after centuries of strife. The struggle
cost many a judge his office, not a few lawyers their lives, and was not won until it had
taken the king's head.

The jurists always labored against great
odds. The king was in a powerful position.
The influence of the church with all its reli-

gious appeal was usually with him. His ancient claim of divine right had been reinforced by the customs and practices of feudalism. Tribal instincts and generations of habit supported him. He was the authority for "the king's peace." There was magic in the name. Moreover, he was always surrounded by powerful ministers, selected from the church and from the legal profession itself. Servile lawyers could always be found to defend his encroachments of power. That this was so, the profession must admit with shame; but that it was not universally so is to the profession's eternal credit. The work of such reactionary ministers was temporary and particular. The continuous influence of the profession as a whole was delivered in support of the law. The glory of the profession lies in the fact that it continued to raise up leaders who opposed the arbitrary will of the kings even when it was supported by men of their own training.

The greatest obstacle to the jurists, however, was found, not in the power of the king, but in the character of their own profession. Because they professed the law, they had to recognize the king whom they opposed as the head of the system which they professed. Because the king was the chief executive officer of the law they had to defer to the office while they defied the incumbent. This circumstance caused a peculiar irony and agony of fate. The supreme sacrifice of the jurist lay not in the fact that he offered his head on the block, but in the paradox that he who was the only loyal champion of the true civil order of the state should be compelled to die under the charge of treason.

The ultimate victory of the profession, however, might have been foretold at the start. It was implicit in the very willingness of the jurists to accept their fate. The attitude of the profession is exemplified in the conduct of one of its great heroes. Sir Thomas More had been made Lord Chancellor by Henry VIII. It was a signal honor, for the office had formerly been given, with three exceptions, only to ecclesiastics. He succeeded Cardinal Wolsey in fame and fate. More held the honor only a short time. Because he strongly disapproved of the divorce of the king from Queen Catherine and the divorce of the Church of England from what he considered the one and only Catholic Church, he resigned and retired to his home at Chelsea. Being a true lawyer, he would not at the king's behest attempt to bend the law to abet a wrong. Henry, however, would not allow him to be forgotten. He was summoned to Lambeth to take the oaths that acknowledged Henry head of the church and pledged obedience to the Act of Succession which promised the crown to the offspring of Anne Boleyn. On his way from Chelsea to Lambeth he was heard by his attendants to say: "I thank our Lord the field is won." They did not then know what he meant. But when they heard of his firm refusal, his dignified farewell to the judges who had convicted him of treason, his noble bearing before his executioner, they knew that the victory which he had won was within himself. His sense of right had prevailed over his love of office, it next prevailed over his love of life. Having "set the world at nought," he had nought to fear from a king. The power of the crown was impotent against men imbued with such a transcendent spirit of victory. Kings and their paramours may prevail for a time, but eventually the world is ruled by the issue and principles of those men who espouse the

law. In this general sense, as well as in a
more particular sense, Coke's quotation from
Fortescue is very apt: "The blessing of
Heaven specially descends upon the posterity
of a great lawyer."

X.

THE CORRUPTION OF THE JUDICIARY

THE legal profession and the crown had not
always been opposed to each other. Kings
and churchmen sometimes furthered and
sometimes opposed the purposes of the profession. The leaders of the bench and bar
worked with them when they were for and
against them when they were against the
principles of the common law. The professional influence was mainly with the king
while he was building a uniform and central-
ized system out of the conflicting mass of local customs and local courts. They worked
together in divesting the church courts of
temporal jurisdiction. By supplanting the
judges educated in the canon or civil law
with judges trained in the common law, their
efforts were united in delivering the courts of

England from the predominance of Rome. But the profession and the crown were set asunder when the Tudor and Stuart rulers began to use the courts as instruments of their tyranny.

The administration of justice in England had from earliest times been most intimately associated with, if not incidental to, the collection of the king's revenue. The people paid taxes in order that the king's peace might be maintained, but the kings maintained the peace in order that taxes could be collected. The judges of assize were for generations the assessors and collectors of taxes. Through the elaborate system of fines and forfeitures Englishmen paid dearly for crude justice. Law for profit never gives real justice. The crown, always pressed for funds to maintain its position at home and prosecute its wars abroad, came to look upon the courts as a chief source of income. We should therefore not be surprised to learn that the judicial office itself was sometimes sold. It too frequently went to the man who would pay for appointment. The amount paid was usually referred to as a contribution to some urgent need of the crown; but this subterfuge served, not so much to disguise the offense, as to expose the offender's consciousness of guilt.

The practice grew so prevalent, it seems, that the exception became remarkable. James I always referred to Judge Nichols as "the judge that would give no money." Now it is invariably true that when an office must be paid for, the incumbent reimburses himself from the office. The judges who paid did not scruple to receive bribes for places which they in turn had to fill. Some took pay for their influence in securing the appointment of others, and some were even paid for pardons which they had authority to grant.

It seems that what the gods would destroy they first make commercial. Cupidity always corrupts. When gain becomes man's goal, the divine incentive of the artist and of the scientist is gone. When man is actuated by avarice, the professional principle can no longer prevail. It is needless to say that these practices produced no great lawyers or judges. John Maxcy Zane refers to the Tudor-Stuart period as The Iron Age, "the saddest in the history of the law." Men truly great and good whose term extended into this age had

a hard time to withstand its evil influences.
Dyer and Coke barely escaped. Bacon's glorious name must bear the stain of impeachment. When the kings learned that there
were lawyers who would pay, they were encouraged to ask more. Judicial appointments
were then usually given to those who would
pledge themselves to royal designs. Judicial
tenure became very dependent upon subserviency to the wishes of the executive.

The shameless oppression which this judicial sycophancy produced or permitted is
now familiar but still disgusting history. The
high tide of tyranny is found in the bloody
records of the state trials of the reigns of
Henry VIII and Elizabeth. These lustful
sovereigns with the aid of their obsequious
ministers of the Star Chamber developed a
very artful system for murder by pretense of
law. The charges of treason, though gro-
tesque in form, were gruesome in effect. "The
wrath of the prince is death" became a phrase
of the time. And nothing was so provocative
of the royal wrath as to thwart the lust of
Prince Henry or to arouse the jealousy of
Princess Elizabeth. Much domestic discord
and many legal entanglements could have

been avoided if Henry's paramours could
have read some premonition of their own future in the fate of their predecessors! But
lovers cannot see. So the continuous wedding
procession of his reign, headed by the heads-
man, continued to lead purblind brides from
marriage to divorce, from altar to block. And
a pandering court set precedents which
daughter Elizabeth found very convenient
when she wished to dispose of ministers who
married or favorites who were so indiscreet
as to become reconciled to their wives.

The religious disputes of the time tended
further to corrupt the courts. The Reforma-
tion of the church led to the confiscation of
church property. Thomas Audley, More's
successor as chancellor, sponsored the legislation and took his share of the plunder. He
robbed the church and debased the human
conscience. He imposed upon Englishmen the
most contradictory oaths. To save their lives
they had to acknowledge the Roman Catholic faith and at the same time accept Henry
as head of the English church. Henry's divorce from Anne of Cleves and marriage to
Catherine Howard was celebrated by burn-
ing at the same fire some Protestants who de-

nied the pope's doctrines and some Catholics who denied the king's supremacy. Church controversies are always cruel. The lust of Henry and the jealousy of Elizabeth were rivaled for cruelty by the bitter bigotry of Mary. The poor judges had a hard time shifting their faith to continue in favor with shifting sovereigns. One of them, Sir James Hale, who had been Protestant under Henry, became Catholic under Mary; but his recantation so preyed upon his conscience that he drowned himself. It was some mark of refinement, even though an indication of weakness, that Hale was unable to endure the evil of the world. Suicide can hardly be justified; but one wonders if it was any more destructive of self for Hale to escape the evil of the world in death than for his confreres to succumb to it in life. The glory of course goes to him who transcends it. The judges who succumbed decided that the judge who escaped had thereby forfeited his estate to the king—and their legal subtleties no doubt further ingratiated them with the crown. The judges who were to transcend the crown were soon to come.

XI.

THE KING UNDER GOD AND THE LAW

In Rome the spirit of the profession preserved the law from the evil influence of the system by which judges were elected. In England it elevated the law above the sinister influence of the system by which judges were appointed. In republican Rome the law was saved from the demoralization of pandering politicians. In monarchical England it was saved from the domination of arbitrary kings.

During the whole period of the Tudor and Stuart reigns the administration of the common law was continuing to develop in spite of prevalent corruption. The evil influence of the crown, like that of the Roman emperors, was largely confined to trials involving political or crown issues. As between one private citizen and another, there was no incentive to interfere, and the law was permitted to work toward even-handed justice. James Dyer, for instance, presided in the Court of Common Pleas for twenty-three years and took no part in the disgraceful state trials. He directed the affairs of the court with efficiency and learning, and began to develop an accurate system of reporting cases. The services of such men acquainted the people with the possibilities of sound legal administration and brought their sentiments to the support of the judiciary.

The courts of general jurisdiction, indeed, had developed such an independent character and devotion to the common law that the crown could not trust them to carry out its purposes. For many years those courts had been showing a disposition to hold officers of the crown to strict accountability for any act which exceeded the letter of the law. The Court of King's Bench had punished a sheriff for failure to execute one of its writs, in spite of the fact that the sheriff had received a letter from the king exonerating the persons against whom the writ was issued, and commanding the sheriff not to take any action against them. The court held that the sheriff could not justify his refusal to perform an order of the court by showing a mere private letter from the king. (A noble precedent for the courts of today!) The court recognized that the king under the law might pardon

offenders, but he might not instruct a sheriff
to disobey the precepts of the law. If he did,
the sheriff could not defend his disobedience
by such an unwarranted act.

Because of such independence in the Courts
of Common Pleas and King's Bench, the
crown tried to establish its absolute sovereignty by creating and extending the jurisdiction of special courts such as the High
Commission, the Court of Requests, and the
Star Chamber. These courts were presided
over by the king's ministers and privy coun-
cilors and assumed the ancient personal jurisdiction of the sovereign. They expanded
the jurisdiction long existent in the King's
Council. The Court of Requests devoted itself to civil causes, the Star Chamber to
criminal cases. The High Commission, established as an administrative tribunal for the
regulation of the church, extended its influence to temporal matters and lay offenders.
Originally such courts had accomplished a
great deal of good. They had punished corruption of sheriffs, bribery of jurors, and
regulated riots and unlawful assemblies.
They assisted in developing the chancery
practice. In England as in Rome there had to

be some means of relief against rigid forms and set writs. Through these special courts and the chancellor, equity again came to the relief of those suitors who were denied justice under the old law. But because of their close association with the crown such special courts became instruments of tyranny. The kings through them tried to subvert the common law courts entirely. The final struggle between the crown and the common law was brought about by the collision between these different courts as well as by the quarrel between king and parliament.

The struggle reached its climax in the life of Sir Edward Coke. James I was king and Coke was chief justice. Whether man makes the place or the place makes the man cannot be definitely determined. But it can be stated quite definitely, as Bacon, Coke's great rival, said when he read the report of the Overbury case, "Never man's person and his place were better met in business than my Lord Coke and my Lord Chief Justice." It may be said of Coke, as truly as of any man that ever lived, that he was the personification of the law. He gave his life to the study of the law and strenuously devoted his knowledge to the liberty and security of his country. Because he was wise and disciplined and uncompromising he seemed to some too harsh and uncongenial. Lord Campbell refers to him as "a deep but narrow-minded lawyer, knowing hardly anything beyond the wearisome and crabbed learning of his own craft . . . and repelling all friendship or attachment by his harsh manners. . . . He never betrayed a friend, or truckled to an enemy. He never tampered with the integrity of judges, or himself took a bribe." He was clean in his person and in his conduct, and dignified in his bearing. He seemed harsh toward those whom he was against and indulgent to those who sought his support. So seems the law always, especially when we look back upon it. He, like the law he championed, became the sword of freedom and the shield of civil order.

When the Court of High Commission, in accordance with the king's notion that his will was absolute law, began to arrest men without formal charge or indictment, imprison them without hearing, try them without fixed rules of procedure, and give judgment without right of appeal, Lord Coke and

his brethren of the Common Pleas bench determined that the High Commission had no
such power in law. They repeatedly issued
writs of prohibition and fearlessly stopped
proceedings which the king was known to
favor.

It was then proposed by one of the king's
ministers, Archbishop Bancroft, that the king
should judge whatever cause he pleased in
his own person, free from all risk of prohibition or appeal. This proposal brought the
executive power of the state and the restrain-
ing power of the law into direct opposition.
The king summoned the judges and his council before him at Whitehall on a Sunday
morning to discuss the proposal. The discussion was opened by the archbishop who said
that the judges were but the delegates of his
majesty and administered the law in his name.
He concluded that what could be done by
the agent could be done by the principal and
that therefore the king might take from the
judges whatever causes it pleased him to determine. He cited as his authority "the Word
of God in the Scriptures." Chief Justice Coke
replied that by the law of England the king
in his own person could not adjudge any case,

but that such matters ought to be determined in some court of justice, and he cited as his authority the Year Books, the early statutes, and Magna Charta, concluding thus: "From a roll of parliament in the Tower of London, 17 Richard II., it appears that a controversy of land between the parties having been heard by the king, and sentence having been given, it was reversed for this,—that the matter belonged to the Common Law." And then ensued the following classic dialogue between the king and the chief justice:

King James: "My Lords, I always thought, and by my saul I have often heard the boast, that your English law was founded upon reason. If that be so, why have not I and others reason as well as you the judges?"

Coke, C. J.: "True it is, please your Majesty, that God has endowed your Majesty with excellent science as well as great gifts of nature; but your Majesty will allow me to say, with all reverence, that you are not learned in the laws of this your realm of England, and I crave leave to remind your Majesty that causes which concern the life or inheritance, or goods or fortunes, of your subjects are not to be decided by natural reason, but by the artificial reason and judgment of law, which law is an art which requires long study and experience before that a man can attain to the cognizance of it. The

law is the golden met-wand and measure to try the
causes of your Majesty's subjects, and it is by the
law that your Majesty is protected in safety and
peace."

King James (in a great rage): "Then I am to be
under the law—which it is treason to affirm."

Coke, C. J.: "Thus wrote Bracton, 'Rex non debet
esse sub homine, sed sub DEO ET LEGE.' " [The
king should not be under man, but under God and
the law.]

The report does not indicate that Coke said
more, but he might well have quoted (if he
had dared) the rest of the passage from Bracton. The following sentence was freighted
with significance, as subsequent events
proved. Bracton had concluded: "Let the
king therefore give to the law what the law
gives to him, dominion and power; for there
is no king where will, and not law, bears
rule." The king might have saved himself
and his successor great woe if he could only
have accepted the truth of that sentence. And
the great world today might still save itself
unutterable distress and woe if it could only
learn that there is not only no king but no
government "where will, and not law, bears
rule."

XII.

A JUDGE LOSES HIS OFFICE,
A KING HIS HEAD

The report of the conference between the king and the judges created a profound impression on the public mind. The king, however, was not diverted by Coke's logic. He soon learned by experience, nevertheless, that the chief justice was right as to the requirement of special learning. After hearing a few cases he was so perplexed that he gave up the business. He said: "I could get on very well hearing one side only, but when both sides have been heard, by my saul I know not which is right."

The ordinary court, therefore, under the leadership of Coke continued to issue writs of prohibition and thus gave a serious check to the arbitrary proceedings of the special courts. King James, however, had begun to issue proclamations whenever he thought that the existing law required amendment. These the common law courts refused to recognize. Again the king summoned a conference to determine whether this power did not by law belong to him. And at this conference Coke announced that "the king cannot, without parliament, change any part of the Common Law, nor create any offense by his proclamation which was not an offense before."

The king at this time also resorted to the practice of issuing orders to the judges to delay proceedings in cases in which he was interested until they had consulted him and obtained his views and wishes. But the judges could not concede this power to the crown either. Coke therefore penned, and he and all the judges signed, a bold but respectful letter in which, after some preliminary statements, they said: "We hold it therefore our duty to inform your Majesty that our oath is in these express words, 'That in case any letter come to us contrary to law we do nothing therefore but certify your Majesty thereof, and go forth to do the law notwithstanding the same.'" This put the king in a great rage. He summoned the judges before him and told them he "approved of their letter neither in its matter nor manner of expression." At the conclusion of the king's statement the judges knelt and prayed for pardon, but Coke, while he expressed deep sorrow for having failed in form, still manfully contended that "obedience to his Majesty's command to stay proceedings would have been a delay of justice, contrary to law, and contrary to the oaths of the judges."

The king was ardently supported at this conference by Lord Chancellor Ellesmere and Attorney General Bacon who insisted that the judges by refusing to comply with the king's request had encroached upon the prerogative royal and had "highly outraged their character." The king said that the attorney general and the chancellor were right and that he would like to know what further could be said in defense of such conduct. Coke thereupon replied: "It would not become me further to argue with your Majesty." All who were present felt that Coke had been effectually humbled and thereupon the following question was put to the judges: "In a case where the king believes his prerogative or interest concerned, and requires the judges to attend him for their advice, ought they not to stay proceedings till his Majesty has consulted them?" All the judges save Coke answered "Yes." Coke said: "When the case happens, I shall do that which shall be fit for a judge to do." The reaction of those present to that simple but sublime answer lends credit to English character. One reads with justifiable pride that the noble bearing of the chief justice abashed the attorney general and commanded the respect of the king himself. The king dismissed them all with a command to keep the limits of their several courts.

Coke was not permitted to retain his office for long, however. With the envy of Bacon and the ill will of other ministers against him, he could not maintain a position in the king's favor. At this time a vacancy occurred in the clerkship of the court, and the king's favorite, the Duke of Buckingham, who was anxious for power and patronage, wished to name the successor. This Coke would not permit but insisted that it was the right of the judges to fill the offices of the court. This display of spirit following his other independent acts was more than the ministers could stand. They determined that Coke should be removed. He was summoned before the Privy Council and charged with misconduct and breach of duty. Lord Campbell says: "Nothing could be more creditable to the nobility and integrity of Coke than the wretched inventions which were resorted to as pretexts for disgracing him." The king yielded to the importunities of his ministers and sent a *supersedeas* to Coke in the following words: "For certain causes now moving us, we will that you shall be no longer our Chief Justice to hold pleas before us, and we command you that you no longer interfere in that office, and by virtue of this presence we at once remove and exonerate you from the same."

This order greatly distressed Coke at the time. But it served a very good purpose for posterity. It removed him from the court where he had already set up the true standards of the law, and enabled him to return to parliament where the battle between the king and the law was thereafter to be more important. Although at first he retired to his private estate and gave his attention to his legal writing, he soon found himself again on the front. He was too strong a character to be permitted to stand idly by while men were fighting for their legal rights.

In parliament he at once became the leader of the opposition to the arbitrary power of the crown. His legal mind analyzed the proposals of the king's ministers into their true significance, and exposed their sinister purpose. When the House was in danger of being misled by high-sounding but vain phrases, he would bring them back to the true course. A writer of the time portrayed the response of parliament to one of his proposals in a characteristic English simile: "This was entertained and answered with a full acclamation of the House—as when one good hound recovers the scent, the rest come in with full cry."

He kept the real issue before the representatives of the people and rallied them to its support by apt quotations from the common law. "The King's answer is very gracious," said he, "but we have to look to the law of the realm." He insisted that messages of love have no lasting endurance in parliament: "Not that I distrust the King, but that I cannot take his trust save in a parliamentary way." He proposed and drafted and presented the Petition of Rights. This act alone well supports the judgment of the constitutional historian that "he became the strenuous asserter of liberty on the principles of those ancient laws which no one was admitted to know so well as himself."

Coke died in the eighty-third year of his life. But the causes which he announced so clearly and championed so bravely continued to be, and still are, vital forces in Anglo-American affairs. The work which Coke could not continue was taken up by other members of the profession. The bar was sufficiently independent to hold out against the attempts of Charles I to raise revenue without act of parliament; the courts ruled that a commitment specifying no offense was illegal; they prohibited torture of prisoners; and held that a defendant could not be compelled to give testimony against himself. The House of Commons organized an army to defend its members whom the king came in person to arrest—with arms but without warrant. Those principles which King James told Coke it was treason to announce, his successor King Charles was told it was treason to deny. The common law had grown so much stronger than the sovereign will in the affections of Englishmen that what the chief justice had been deposed for proclaiming the king was beheaded for disclaiming.

XIII.

AN INDEPENDENT COURT

BUT the victory for the law was not so immediate as that statement would indicate. Too often people who depose tyrants find that they have merely exchanged tyrants. The leaders of parliament and the army became as autocratic as the king's ministers had been. And as usual they based their arbitrary power upon the same authority. As we have seen, King James's assumption of supreme judicial authority was based upon "the Word of God in the Scriptures"; and Bradshaw, who presided over the court that condemned King Charles to death, said it acted by "God's authority and the kingdom's."

But these assumptions, like the attempt to substitute the law of Moses for the common law, did not last long. The pressure of the profession was continuously against them. The jurists kept up the struggle for the orderly processes of the law in spite of shifting rulers. The men who had declaimed against King Charles's ship money as vigorously denounced Cromwell's arbitrary taxation. But the Protector equaled the kings in disdain for courts and lawyers. In true regal fashion he sent for Chief Justice Rolle and his brethren of the bench when they attempted to try the legality of his tax and roundly reprehended them. He spoke with contempt of their Magna Charta, and said they should not permit lawyers to prate about things that it ill became them to hear. Prynne and Maynard who had argued against the tax were fined and imprisoned. But the profession was never repressed. When Cromwell's officers attempted to intimidate Sir Matthew Hale for his defense of Lord Capel and the Duke of Hamilton, he replied that while doing his duty to clients and supporting the law he would not be daunted by threats. The courts did not hesitate to bring to trial and condemn one of Cromwell's soldiers for the murder of a Royalist or to quash a panel of jurors returned at Cromwell's order.

So the contest between arbitrary will and common law continued through Commonwealth and Restoration. The return of the Stuart kings brought a revival of bad practices. Charles II and James II profited nought by the experience of Charles I. Neither were they impressed by the more favorable experience of the older Lancastrian rulers who had respected the law and generally upheld the independence of judges. They ruthlessly cleared the courts of the judges who would not do their bidding. King James II had the audacity to call upon the judges again to hold that the king by proclamation could set aside the acts of parliament. The judges again refused. The king removed them from office saying that he was determined to have twelve lawyers for judges, all of his way of thinking. To this Chief Justice Jones replied: "Your Majesty may find twelve judges of your mind, but never twelve lawyers."

Public sentiment against the king was so strong that finally he had to flee to France, and with him went the doctrine as to the supreme power of the prince. It could not prevail against the Anglo-Saxon love of law. Through all vicissitudes the independent administration of justice had been steadily developing. Not only the judges but the jury also had been made more independent. The practice of fining and imprisoning jurors for what was conceived to be a false verdict was abolished. The courts, however, were given power to grant new trials in case of erroneous verdicts. Rules for the admission of testimony were established to the end that prejudicial considerations might be excluded from the jury. The jury was required to determine its verdict from evidence offered in open court under the direction of the judge. Jury duty, moreover, had been familiarizing laymen with the character of the English courts.

A king in Bracton's day could say with impunity to one of his judges: "I raised you from the depths, you were the scribbler of my writs, a justice and a hireling." By Coke's time the judicial position had been strengthened to such extent that a judge could tell the king that he was under God and the law. When the king persisted in the assertion of his arbitrary will, however, the judge of Coke's time had to admit: "It would not become me further to argue with your Majesty." But by the time of James II the chief justice could say to the king quite frankly that he was mortified that His Majesty could think him capable of a judgment which none but an ignorant or dishonest man could give.

With the removal of the last of the Stuarts the independence of the judicial officers was established. From that time judges have held their office during good behavior, not during the pleasure of the crown. Since the revolution of 1688 there has not been a removal of a judge by executive order, nor has there been known a single instance of a corrupt decision. The last faltering attempt to control the administration of justice by political pressure was made during the reign of William III. A ministry tried to coerce justices of the peace by the power of dismissal from office but there was such a storm of opposition that no later ministry has dared to make such an attempt.

Through the centuries, by patient perseverance in spite of constant opposition and numerous reverses, the legal profession led in the effort to establish the conception of law as reason above the idea of law as will. That the profession is entitled to principal praise for the accomplishment is not only shown by the record of their performances but proved by the application of an old adage. It has been well said that the tree that bears the best fruit is indicated by the number of clubs found under it. The historic ground under the legal tree is covered with base epithets and invectives hurled against it by kings and ministers and prelates who claimed special privileges. "No man e'er felt the halter draw, with good opinion of the law." Those persons who have felt the pressure of the law against their selfish interests have been loud in their denunciation of the profession. As the lawyers of Rome gave us the science of law, the lawyers of England gave us the science of administering the law, and their principal contribution to that end was an independent court.

An ancient legend comes down to us from the reign of Henry IV. The Prince of Wales, though brave and generous, is said to have been wild and dissipated, and very much devoted to his dissolute companions. When Gascoigne, chief justice of the King's Bench, was called upon to impose a penalty upon one of those companions for some depredation, the Prince of Wales drew his sword and threatened the chief justice. For this act of violence the chief justice ordered the prince to prison. The prince, having recovered his mental poise, submitted in good grace to the order of the court. The king, when he heard of this incident, is reported to have exclaimed: "Happy is the monarch who has so just a

judge, and a son so willing to obey the law."
The experience of England with its independent judiciary has now enabled the world to say: "Happy is the nation which has just judges and sons so willing to obey the law."

Through England's numerous colonies Anglo-Saxon jurisprudence has had an influence in the world more extensive than Roman jurisprudence, even if not so general. One historian has referred to England as a nation "marked for a sturdy sense of right," and English rule has generally justified the comment. Men of other nationalities have spoken in high praise of the veracity and fairness of the men whom England has entrusted with the administration of the law. Sven Hedin, the great Swedish explorer, has borne testimony to the high character of English legal administration even at its outposts. And men of other countries have frequently gone into England to submit their controversies with Englishmen to the judgment of English courts, as did His Excellency Chang Yen Mao, of China, in his suit against Moreing and others. English courts generally have justified the faith of the stranger, as did Mr. Justice Joyce in the case mentioned. It can be said by an American jurist that the English judiciary has no superior among the courts of the world, because English judges have understood the universality of the law and have demonstrated their patriotism, not by chauvinism, but by their devotion to truth and justice.

PART THREE

THE SPIRIT OF THE LEGAL PROFESSION

IN AMERICA

XIV.

LAWYERS AND THE REVOLUTION

BECAUSE of the sense of right and the respect for law which have marked the Anglo-Saxon race generally, the English dominion became divided into two parts. It was owing to their inherited devotion to these principles that the American colonies separated themselves from the rest of the British Empire. And it was due to that same devotion to law that the separate colonies were able to weld themselves into one nation. The establishment of an independent nation in America was not so much a revolution as it was a continued assertion or evolution of the racial convictions and deep-seated loyalties that had been asserting themselves in England for centuries. And it is quite probable that the same devotion to law will again unite England and America in the defense of those racial convictions against the forms of absolutism that threaten them today.

After the Restoration the British kings continued to assert against the colonists the

arbitrary power which their predecessors had
tried to impose upon the men of England.
But the colonies, having been founded largely
by men in rebellion against such oppression,
continued the struggle against the imperious
will of the sovereign, without the abatement
that occurred in England under the Hano-
verian rulers. The Puritan influence, which
had waned in England, continued strong in
America. The opposition in England to taxes
imposed by the crown became in America opposition to "taxation without representa-
tion." The sentiment in England against the
despotic orders of the Star Chamber and
High Commission reasserted itself in the
colonial Resolves "that all trials for any
crime whatsoever should be within the colony
by known course of law." The authority of
the king in the colonies became a prime issue
on both sides of the ocean. The king's party,
so far as the American issue was concerned,
won in England, but it lost in America. That
the colonists were continuing the struggle for
the establishment of the law is shown by the
fact that they were championed on both sides
by the ablest lawyers. The rights of the colonies were defended in England by Sir Rob-

ert Walpole, Edmund Burke, William Pitt,
Charles James Fox, and others. In America
the rebellion was led by men who personified
the spirit of the profession.

The "First Act in the American Revolution" was the opposition of James Otis to the
"writs of assistance," which were warrants
for the seizure of goods merely suspected of
being contraband. Otis had been king's advocate in the province of Massachusetts, but resigned to appear in court against such unlawful warrants. The use of such writs, he argued, was an act of tyranny similar to the
abuse of power which had "cost one king of
England his head, another his throne." He
based his arguments upon the teachings of
Coke (who, we have seen, had based his arguments against similar usurpation of power
upon the teachings of Bracton), and he held
that the acts providing for such writs, being
against the Constitution of England, were
void. His speech had a wonderful effect upon
the popular mind. Our report of it is contained in the notes made by John Adams,
then a student of law in Boston.

Thus was the young lawyer inspired who
in his day was to become so stalwart a leader

in the same cause—who was in time to nominate Washington as Commander in Chief of the Colonial forces and John Marshall as Chief Justice of the Supreme Court!

In Virginia the people were being aroused by the oratory of Patrick Henry, a well-educated young lawyer, who "had been admitted to the bar because of his knowledge of English constitutional history." He had argued in The Parson's Cause that government was a conditional compact between the king and the people, and that the veto by the king of an act passed by the Virginia Assembly for the benefit of the people was a violation of that compact. The king, he said, had "degenerated into a tyrant and forfeited all right to his subjects' obedience."

His views and his courage made him popular and he was made a member of the House of Burgesses. He sponsored the resolutions opposing the Stamp Act. The Burgesses affirmed the right of the colonists to be governed by their own Assembly in the matter of taxes and internal police. This and similar opposition in the other colonies led, on motion of James Otis of Massachusetts, to the

Stamp Act Congress, to which all the colonies except New Hampshire sent delegates. For years the British Government had been endeavoring to unite the colonies in opposition to the French, but without success. Now the colonies came together of their own accord to defend their lawful rights. They passed resolutions acknowledging their allegiance to the crown but declaring themselves entitled to all the liberties of "natural born subjects in Great Britain." They opposed the peremptory jurisdiction of the admiralty courts under the Stamp Act and affirmed "that trial by jury is the inherent and invaluable right of every British subject."

This united effort taught the colonies the need of holding annual intercolonial congresses. To the first Continental Congress the colonies sent their ablest lawyers: John Adams from Massachusetts, Judge Stephen Hopkins from Rhode Island, Roger Sherman from Connecticut, John Jay from New York, John Dickinson from Pennsylvania, John Rutledge from South Carolina, Patrick Henry, Richard Henry Lee, and Peyton Randolph from Virginia. A number of the delegates had been educated in England, some in the Inns of Court. Jay and Rutledge afterwards became Chief Justices of the Supreme Court of the United States. The prominence of the lawyers who attended is indicated by the statement of a noted historian, who, after noting that Franklin and Jefferson were not delegates to the first Continental Congress, says, "With those exceptions, all the ablest men then in political life were present."

The quarrel of the separate colonies with England made necessary some new provisions for local government. The departure of royal governors, which had left some colonies without any government, and the resistance to royal charters in other provinces, required new arrangements for civil order. Such conditions afforded rare experience in the science of government. The colonies were training schools for the nation soon to be. The men who distinguished themselves in public affairs at home were then sent as delegates to the Continental Congress. The first Congress, like the Stamp Act Assembly, acted only in an advisory capacity. But the Second Continental Congress began to exercise sovereign powers. It assumed the defense of the colonies, supported an army, issued paper money to pay its soldiers, drew regulations for its own government, established a Committee of Correspondence, and took exclusive charge of foreign affairs. The king's refusal to consider the "Olive Branch" petition and his employment of Hessian soldiers to fight his own subjects forced the colonies into open rebellion against England and into alliance with France. Virginia instructed her delegates in Congress to propose a declaration of independence. A committee of five was appointed for the purpose: Thomas Jefferson, Benjamin Franklin, John Adams, Roger Sherman, and Robert Livingston. All except Franklin were lawyers. Jefferson's previous experience in drafting the Virginia declaration marked him as the man best fitted to formulate our national birth certificate. Of the fifty-six men who signed the Declaration of Independence more than half were lawyers. It is the very essence of the spirit of law, and exemplifies the virtue of professional training—it is a pronouncement of political principles; a denunciation of wrongs; an affirmation of justice and freedom founded upon a broad philosophy and deep religious sensibility; and expressed in language dignified, clear, and concise.

Independence having been proclaimed, many of the lawyers left the legislative halls to defend the new nation. General Washington drew from the profession some of his ablest aides. Some distinguished themselves as military commanders. While the principal object of the law is peace and order, yet lawyers as a class have not blinked the fact that at times it can be realized only by force. The goddess of justice has always been portrayed with the scales in one hand and the sword in the other. No true lawyer would allow her to be disarmed. No jurist worthy of his calling has ever permitted sophistry or sentimentality to deter the enforcement of a just judgment. One of the chief purposes of the law is to make the lawless conform. As Maitland has said, "Laws have need of arms: Justinian knew it well." The justification of the lawyer's resort to arms is found in the righteousness of the cause he espouses and the promptness with which he lays arms down when his duty is done.

XV.

COLONISTS AVERSE TO LAWYERS

IT would be a mistake to assume from what has been said that lawyers had held a prominent place in colonial affairs from the beginning. It is indeed a rather common error to think that the colonists brought with them the common law and a regard for all its institutions. But the contrary is the truth. There was a strong aversion to the law and to lawyers in the early life of all the colonies. The history of law in England had to be repeated in New England. A system of law, as well as independent courts for its administration, had again to be provided—and again they came at the cost of patient effort and heroic sacrifice. They came in answer to an inherent need of society—and again the need was met by men imbued with the spirit of the profession.

It was of course impossible for the settlers to cut themselves loose from their past experience. Their familiarity with law and legal practice came with them to their new home and continued to color their thinking.

The more general and popular parts of the common law were for that reason of great influence on colonial legal relations. But the common law was not at first accepted as law in America. It was not even recognized as a subsidiary system. In many of the colonies religious feeling was so intense and general that no law was considered necessary other than that found in the Scriptures. In Massachusetts it was provided that "the judges have power to inflict penalties according to the rule of God's word." If the colony had a law on the subject before the court, the judges were constrained to conform their decisions thereto, but where there was no law, "then as near the law of God as they can."

In New Jersey it was enacted that "all persons guilty of murder or treason shall be sentenced by the general assembly, as they in the wisdom of the Lord shall judge meet and expedient." Connecticut also made the Scriptures a guide for judicial decisions. In Virginia the law was administered by the country gentlemen, and their sense of right was their guide. The instruction to the commissioner of monthly courts was: "You shall do equal right to poor and to rich after your cunning, wit and power and after the laws and customs of this colony." In the colonies generally, as to matters not covered by local law, the discretion of the magistrates or judges was relied upon to furnish a rule satisfactory to the popular sense of right.

Such an arrangement was at first quite satisfactory. The life of the earliest settlers was primitive and their social and legal problems very simple. It required no technical training to meet their needs. The population of each province was homogeneous, and an informal administration of law by laymen could meet the general need of justice in the community. So it is easy to understand why the earliest settlers felt no need for lawyers, but it is not so easy to understand why they felt such an aversion to them. They must have associated them with the tyranny from which they had escaped. Too often lawyers and the law are blamed for the errors and misdeeds which fools and tyrants commit under the cloak of the law.

But whatever the cause, the prejudice existed before ever there was a professional class in America. In Massachusetts lawyers were forbidden to practice their profession.

The few men in the colony who had received legal training were compelled, like Letchford, to give their attention to editorial and other work. The feeling toward lawyers in Rhode Island is shown by the fact that the Assembly in 1729 would not permit them to serve as deputies, "their presence being found to be of ill consequence." We read that in New York "the general cry of the people both in town and country was, 'No lawyer in the Assembly!'" In Virginia the inhibition was against the commercialization of the professional relationship. In 1645 an act was passed expelling the mercenary attorneys. Like ancient Rome, Virginia declared that "none shall plead for recompense." At a later period the House of Burgesses passed an act forbidding any person to plead or give advice in any case for reward. In a sense it is a high tribute to the profession that any commercialization of it should be thought so reprehensible. Such a feeling has generally attended a people of high civic consciousness.

Throughout the early colonies men did not hesitate to plead their own causes, unassisted save by the unremunerated help of a friend or by the court itself. The ordinary courts were not presided over by trained judges but by popular representatives who enforced the general sense of right and otherwise exercised an untrammeled discretion. In New Hampshire no real jurist, no man acknowledging a regular development of the law by precedents or accepting any authoritative guidance from the adjudications of the common law, held judicial office during the entire eighteenth century. When Lord Petersborough visited the colony of Pennsylvania he was astonished at "the fewness of laws, the informality of judicial proceedings, and the absence of lawyers." Even in Maryland, where there was a more kindly disposition toward the common law, the opposition to lawyers was quite marked. The profession had to earn its place in America.

XVI.

NEED OF LAW AND INDEPENDENT COURTS

AMERICAN soil was congenial to Anglo-Saxon blood. As soon as the hardships of first settlement were surmounted, life in the colonies expanded rapidly. New industries were created and a very profitable trade between the colonies and with foreign countries was soon developed. Travel and intercommunication increased. New settlers came and the population grew more heterogeneous. Some of the seaports became quite cosmopolitan. As life became more involved and all its relations more complex, the need of a more highly developed legal system became apparent. Social and commercial interests required a more refined legal analysis. We have seen in our own time how increased highway traffic has increased traffic regulations. So it is in all the ways of life. Developments bring complications.

As men's interests were extended their mutual and reciprocal rights and liabilities increased and they therefore had increasing need to know the law. Furthermore, they needed to know it in advance. They began to look to the provisions of the common law— the only law expressed in their own language. The generalities of the pious pioneers were not sufficiently specific to serve as guides. Honest men might differ as to the interpretation of God's word. In relationships so complex all men might not have the same sense of right. In Massachusetts one defendant, after being fined and bound to his good behavior, asked the judges rather pointedly what good behavior was. The uncontrolled discretion of the magistrates and judges began to irk the men who felt the need of certainty. When they sought to clarify conditions by definite enactments in their assemblies, they found that the men who had been interpreting God's word and determining what was right resented such interference with their discretion. Moreover, the colonial governors and their councils also looked with a jealous eye upon any action which they thought might interfere with their royal prerogatives.

Nearly every royal charter vested supreme judicial as well as other authority in the colonial governor or proprietor and his council. Thus the executive, legislative, and judicial functions had again merged—and again men of Anglo-Saxon blood battled for their separation. The arbitrary rule and peremptory writs and orders of the royal governors forced the colonists to assert their rights as Englishmen under English law. They began to speak of Magna Charta, the right of *habeas corpus*, and of trial by jury. They were supported to some extent by the charters themselves. Most of them provided that the colonial government should "be conformable to the laws of England, so far as the nature and constitution of the place will admit," or that it might enact such laws as were "not repugnant to the laws of England."

Not only did the colonists feel a need for the general provisions of the common law to regulate their commercial and social activities and for its fundamental provisions for the protection of their civil liberties, but they also felt an increasing need for the principles of equitable jurisprudence as administered by the courts of England. They found that the limited enactments of their own assemblies and such of the common law principles as had been adopted here were insufficient or too rigorous to meet the requirements of many cases. The obligations of trustees and other fiduciaries had to be enforced. Mistakes were made that required correction. Deeds absolute on their face needed to be interpreted as mortgages or conditional grants.

The evolution of colonial life led again to the requirement of some agency to ameliorate the severity of the law.

Such equitable jurisdiction as had been exercised in the colonies was vested exclusively in the colonial governor and his council. The colonial governor was the keeper of the colonial seal and by analogy to English practice he was therefore considered to be also "the keeper of the king's conscience," which had been considered the source of equitable jurisdiction. But the life of the colonies had expanded far beyond the seat of the governor and his council, and resort to the equitable authority of that court was therefore found to be too arduous and expensive. There came in time to be an insistent demand for more available courts of equitable jurisdiction. In 1705 the Assembly of Rhode Island decided to act as a court of chancery, but six years later it determined that it "had no power or authority to make any such law." It then proceeded to establish "a regular court of chancery, within the government according to the methods and precedents of Great Britain." In the Carolinas a court of chancery was established as early as 1697, in which the English chancery practice was in the main adhered to.

The foremost demand for a definite establishment of law and independent courts was asserted in New York. This was quite natural because there the elements were more diverse and trade more advanced. The House of Assembly resolved that two lawyers be heard in relation to the organization of courts of justice, "as numberless petitions had been presented deploring the condition of the judiciary." In the year 1700 a professional English lawyer, Attwood, became chief justice of New York. The lead which New York then took in adapting the common law to American conditions was maintained until the law was codified. Its great judges like Kent became the authoritative expounders of the American form of the common law.

Massachusetts followed New York. There are definite records of very early complaints against the legal system. In 1646, Robert Child led a party of colonists who petitioned for the establishment of the wholesome laws of England, "which are the result of long ex-

perience and are best agreeable to English
tempers, that there might be a settled rule of
adjudicature from which the magistrates cannot swerve." The general court answered the
petition in dual form; first in a qualified de-
nial and next by way of confession and
avoidance. The court said: "The laws of the
colony are not diametrically opposed to the
law of England for then they must be contrary to the laws of God, on which the Common Law, so far as it is law, is also founded."
They closed by confessing an insufficient
knowledge of the laws of England and said:
"If we had able lawyers amongst us we
might have been more exact." Letchford, in
his book *Plain Dealing*, complained because
the governor in charging the grand jury used
the heads of the Ten Commandments; that
in jury trials matters of law and fact were
not distinguished; that the records of the
courts were not kept in due form of law; that
there was a disposition to slight all former
laws and precedents. He advised the colonists to "despise not learning nor the learned
lawyers of either gown." All this led in 1712
to the appointment of the first professional

lawyer, Lynde, as chief justice, and thereafter we find that English books and authors
were frequently cited.

Although the country fairly "groaned"—
as one governor put it—for regular courts of
law, yet the colonies very generally objected
to the establishment of such courts by order
of the governor. Many of the assemblies resolved that no court could be established
without their consent. The controversy in the
colonies on this point, and particularly the
objections of the colonists to the injunctions
and other orders of the governors which interfered with the work of the courts, sound
like echoes of the controversy between parliament and the kings of England.

Again the movement for law produced
lawyers. The need of a definite establishment
for the administration of justice supplied a
professional class. In the middle of the seven-
teenth century this interest in law created
what one historian refers to as "a custom of
studying law in England." But when relations between England and America became
strained that custom ceased. From that time
the profession continued to develop here as it
had developed in Rome. The older members

acted as tutors to their successors, and their work was facilitated by the publication at that time of Blackstone's Commentaries. Law-office study became the general method of legal instruction. Most of the great lawyers of the formative period of our history received their training in the offices of older lawyers. The best lawyers of that day were not too busy to act as preceptors.

George Wythe of Virginia is the outstanding example of the lawyer-tutor of that time. Although he was a very busy practitioner, served in the Assembly of his state, was a signer of the Declaration of Independence, a member of the Federal Convention that adopted the Constitution, and chancellor of his state, he found time to direct the education of worthy young men. Jefferson, Marshall, and Henry Clay were prepared for the bar in his office. He afterwards became the first college teacher of law in this country. He was made professor of jurisprudence in William and Mary College. He is referred to by the biographer of one of his great students as "one of the most honorably distinguished men of a period abounding in great names." It is recorded that he took a warm and confi-

dential interest in the young student, direct-
ing his reading, "at first turning him to gram-
matical studies, and then gradually opening
to him a wider range of legal and historical
literature." In the pauses of their work and
in hours of leisure he would converse with
the young man on grave subjects, "and thus
did much to direct his thoughts and to form
his principles." Thus we see that the great
lawyers of this country's early history did
not happen by chance. Their training was
thorough and encompassed the ancient traditions of the profession. Here again we ob-
serve that it began with a mastery of the
word and extended to a consideration of the
fundamental principles of life.

XVII.

THE GIFT OF THE
CONSTITUTION

INDEPENDENCE having been established, a
government had to be provided. Man, in the
course of his legal evolution, having produced first a system of law and next a system
of administration, came in time to develop a
new system of government. The law came

from the Latins, the independent judiciary from the Anglo-Saxons, and the new Constitution of government from the New World. "The most wonderful work ever struck off at a given time by the brain and purpose of man" was the gift of America to the world.

For the first time a charter and complete frame of government were encompassed in one document. Theories were reduced to formulae and given practical application. The wisdom of the ages and the experience of all nations were garnered together and crystallized in a brief statement of principles. Thirteen sovereign states were welded into a federal republic. While the local independence of each was preserved, they were bound into an indissoluble union. Governments within a government, overlapping, but each operating in its own sphere! The fundamental and permanent was segregated from the superficial and temporary. The continental and national was distinguished from the local and individual. The basis of government was fixed. The sovereignty of the people was acknowledged and the authority of their agents, the government, was defined and limited. For the first time a tribunal was empowered to interpret such authority and adjudicate its limits.

But Gladstone's famous remark about "the most wonderful work ever struck off at a given time," while perfectly true, is nevertheless misleading. It was made in order to contrast the American Constitution to the British Constitution which, he said, "is the most subtle organism which has proceeded from progressive history." It would, however, be in the highest degree erroneous to suppose that the Constitution of the United States is not, as much as any other, an instance of evolution from precedents. Its comprehensive yet compressed form and some of its provisions were original, but the material of which it was made had come from preceding ages. It is significant that the members of the Convention are usually referred to as Framers of the Constitution. The term seems to concede that the Convention merely assembled the parts that had been fabricated by previous political processes. The raw material of the Constitution had been in process of manufacture for many years. The heat and force which had created it and which now molded it into new form were generated mainly by the spirit of the legal profession.

It would be too much to say that the Constitution was exclusively the work of lawyers. In the field of public law there has always been a prominent place for laymen and specialists from other vocations. If the work in that field were left entirely to lawyers it might become too highly specialized and technical and lose its common touch and practical value. The contribution of men like Washington and Franklin to the Constitution can hardly be overestimated. They took the place in American history which the bishops and barons had occupied in English history. Washington's was no doubt the strongest individual influence. Without his help it is inconceivable that the Constitution could have been adopted at that time. His particular contribution, however, was his influence upon the public and the other members of the Convention. The detail work of formulating the Constitution and of presenting it to the people was done by lawyers. James Madison of Virginia, a student of law and constitutional history, is generally re-

ferred to as "The Father of the Constitution." Certainly he and Alexander Hamilton, a lawyer from New York, were the most
profound and original thinkers in the Convention. John Fiske says: "These two men
must be ranked in the same order with Aris-
totle, Montesquieu and Locke; and the 'Federalist,' their joint production, is the greatest
treatise on government that has ever been
written."

For fourteen years—from the Declaration
of Independence to the ratification of the
Constitution by the thirteenth state (Rhode
Island, 1790)—the front line positions in
the battle for a stronger federal government
were occupied by lawyers. It was more than
a battle—it was a war. It required consum-
mate skill, heroic courage, and sublime patience. The whole trend of public opinion
had to be changed. The colonists had labored
so arduously for freedom that they were loath
to surrender any of it. They were suspicious
of a strong central government. The bonds of
England had been cast off; why should they
forge new ones? Hamilton had expressed the
belief that, "very little would be done till the
entire change of the present system," and, be-

fore that could be effected, "mountains of prejudice and particular interest were to be levelled." It was no job for demagogues and followers. It was a work for leaders and statesmen.

The lawyers of the various states continually pressed the need of a stronger union upon their own people, and their local efforts were drawn into a national movement under the great personality of Washington. The first convention for the purpose of establishing "a congress upon a constitutional footing" was attended by delegates from only the New England states and New York, but the historian records, "The lead in the convention was taken by the delegates from New York, Hobart, a judge of its supreme court, and Benson, its attorney general." When the Continental Congress appointed a committee to "prepare an exposition of the confederation, to devise a plan for its complete execution, and to present supplemental articles," Edmund Randolph of Virginia, Oliver Ellsworth of Connecticut, and James Varnum of Rhode Island were selected—"three of the ablest lawyers in their states." When the Federal Convention that drafted the Consti-

tution finally assembled, no one was surprised
to find that it was "composed chiefly of lawyers." Four of the delegates had studied law
at the Inns of Court. James Wilson of Pennsylvania, "one of the most learned jurists this
country has ever seen," was educated in
Scotland.

The truth of the matter is, the very times
were permeated with the spirit of the law.
By the time of the Federal Convention there
had been developed, by education and by an
increasing sense of need, a passionate yearning for unity and a very general understanding that such unity must be based upon law.
Men who read at all read law. Blackstone's
Commentaries were familiar to many besides
the practitioners. Many of the delegates to
the Convention made a manual of Montesquieu's *The Spirit of Laws*. Washington
with his own hand copied an abstract which
Madison had made of that great work. It is a
significant fact, indicative of the general interest in the great American experiment, that
Montesquieu's grandson came to the aid of
this country, along with other notable
Frenchmen, and won promotion for good
service. The same thing drew him to America

that drew Americans to the work of his grandsire—the Spirit of Law.

The very times, moreover, were imbued with a professional spirit. Selfish and sordid motives did not actuate the men who made this nation. The Constitution could never have been made by little souls—the victims of pride and pelf. The founding fathers were not title-seekers or job-holders. One who reads their private correspondence and public utterances has no doubt that they were conscious of their destiny. They knew they were building a new nation—and they ordered their lives to their calling. Washington's circular letter to the governors of the states, in which he appealed to the whole people for a stronger Constitution, is a clarion call to consecration and service:

. . . This is the moment to give such a tone to our federal government as will enable it to answer the ends of its institution. According to the system of policy the states shall adopt at this moment, it is to be decided whether the Revolution must ultimately be considered as a blessing or a curse; a blessing or a curse, not to the present age alone, for with our fate will the destiny of unborn millions be involved.

Essential to the existence of the United States is the friendly disposition which will forget local prejudices and policies, make mutual concessions to the general prosperity, and, in some instances, sacrifice individual advantages to the interest of the community. . . .

It is indispensable to the happiness of the individual states that there should be lodged somewhere a supreme power to regulate and govern the general concerns of the confederated republic, without which the Union cannot be of long duration, and everything must very rapidly tend to anarchy and confusion. . . . We shall be left nearly in a state of nature; or we may find by our own unhappy experience that there is a natural and necessary progression from the extreme of anarchy to the extreme of tyranny, and that arbitrary power is most easily established on the ruins of liberty abused to licentiousness.

In response to that majestic message, in order to establish the balance of the law between the extremes which Washington feared, the Federal Convention met. Bancroft, in his *History of the Constitution*, thus portrays the feelings of the patriots as they convened:

Discordant passions were repressed by the solemnity of the moment; and, as the statesmen who were to create a new constitution, veterans in the war and in the halls of legislation, journeyed for the most part on horseback to their place of meeting, the high-

wrought hopes of the nation went along with them.
. . . They felt the ennobling love for their fellow-
men, and knew themselves to be forerunners of reform for the civilized world.

And Madison, writing at the close of his
life what Elliot has considered a preface to
his notes on the Convention, said retrospec-
tively:

I feel it a duty to express my profound and solemn
conviction, derived from my intimate opportunity
of observing and appreciating the views of the Convention, collectively and individually, that there
never was an assembly of men, charged with a great
and arduous trust, who were more pure in their motives, or more exclusively or anxiously devoted to
the object committed to them, than were the members of the Federal Convention of 1787 to the object
of devising and proposing a constitutional system
which should best supply the defects of that which
it was to replace, and best secure the permanent
liberty and happiness of their country.

XVIII.

THE JUDICIAL POWER

OUR purpose does not require a discussion of
the Constitution in all its parts, but Article
III which provides for "The Judicial Power

of the United States" deserves special attention. As John Fiske has said:

The federal judiciary was the most remarkable and original of all the creations of that wonderful convention. It was charged with the duty of interpreting, in accordance with the general principles of Common Law, the Federal Constitution itself. This is the most noble as it is the most distinctive feature in the government of the United States.

Most remarkable, next to the provision itself, was the unanimity with which it was adopted. It is almost unbelievable that a convention "composed chiefly of lawyers"— a class not known for tractability—could so readily agree regarding problems which at other times have occasioned such divergence of opinion. All the historians of this period have been impressed by this general agreement. Fiske and Bancroft and Curtis have all commented upon the absence of any disagreement among the delegates as to the judiciary. This was not due to indifference, for the organization of the judiciary engaged the most eager attention of the delegates. They recognized at the time, as historians have conceded since, that to provide a proper judicial system "was by far the most delicate and difficult of their duties." In spite of the persistent efforts for the preservation of states' rights, the resolution for a national judiciary, consisting of one supreme tribunal and one or more inferior tribunals, passed without debate and unanimously. Even the method of choosing the federal judiciary was settled without strife. The motion for its appointment by the executive with the advice and consent of the Senate was finally agreed to without a division.

This consensus can hardly be accounted for except by considering this Article as the logical culmination of the legal history of the race. The men who drafted it were well informed as to that history and had had first-hand experience with the legal evolution of America. The work was done chiefly in committee by Ellsworth, Wilson, Randolph, and Rutledge—four able lawyers. Afterwards Ellsworth became chief justice and Wilson an associate justice of the court they helped to create. The provisions of the article did not differ essentially from the Virginia plan which Randolph had submitted to the Convention and which Madison had helped so materially to form.

The framers of the Constitution recognized that man is a social being and that some civil order is essential to his welfare. As James Wilson said in his great speech recommending ratification of the Constitution by the Pennsylvania Convention, man in a natural state would enjoy less liberty and suffer more interruption than in a regulated society. "Hence," said he, "the universal introduction of governments of some kind or other into the social state. The liberty of every member is increased by this introduction; for each gains more by the limitation of the freedom of every other member, than he loses by the limitation of his own. The result is, that civil government is necessary to the perfection and happiness of man." The framers therefore at the same time that they recognized the sovereignty of the people also recognized the dependence of the people upon government. In other words, it was recognized that the sovereign people were, like Coke's sovereign king, "under God and the law."

As Monroe said, the sovereignty was with the people, but the government was with their agents. Because all authority was derived from the people, it was necessary to classify the agencies of government and specify the authority of each. In order to prevent the abuse of the power which necessarily exists in government, the three main functions of government, legislative, executive, and judicial, were separated and each was made supreme in its sphere and each was balanced against the others. The great sentiment for a stronger central government was based upon the supposition that there would be a Constitution, as Thomas Paine said in his *Common Sense*, "defining and describing the powers of Congress." The defining of one function of course led to the defining of all. That very conception of a defined government required the establishment of an overruling law of laws, the Constitution. The formulation of such a fundamental law led naturally to the establishment of a supreme tribunal for its authentic interpretation, and the whole history of the human race dictated that such a court should be independent. The framers of the Constitution knew the needs of humanity and the purpose of the judicial function. They knew these things so well that they were of one mind concerning them.

A national judiciary was necessary not only to interpret the Constitution and protect persons against abuse of power by government, it was necessary to maintain the balance between the different divisions of government, between the sovereign states, and between the states and the federal government, as well as to adjudicate the causes of foreigners and citizens of different states. If the Constitution and the laws and treaties made in pursuance of its provisions were to be the supreme law of the land, then that supremacy had to be maintained by some department of the national government. If the states themselves should be the final judges of the meaning and operation of the Constitution, its laws and treaties, then the new government would be no stronger than the old Continental Congress. National needs required a national government, but such a government could be established only upon an express charter defining the conditions of its establishment. And such a charter could be agreed upon only if some federal agency could be entrusted with the determination of controversies which were bound to arise under such conditions.

That this transcendent power of interpretation and application, even as it affected the rights and authority of sovereign states and the federal government itself, could be entrusted to the judiciary through judicial process, is due to the social and legal development of that time. The proposal to maintain the national supremacy, within the sphere of national action, by executive or legislative order was made and discussed. But it was promptly conceded that any direct interference would wound and irritate and likely lead to civil strife. Such suggestions as legislative arrest or veto of state laws, executive order, and military force were promptly abandoned. But the doctrine of supremacy of law and the function of an independent judiciary were so well established and highly respected that the makers of the Constitution could now provide that: "The Judicial Power shall extend to all Cases in Law and Equity, arising under this Constitution . . . ; to Controversies to which the United States shall be a Party; to Controversies between two or more States. . . ." To statesmen imbued with the spirit of the legal profession it was not derogatory to the dignity of a state to subject it to the judicial power when that power was to be exercised by an independent tribunal according to the established processes of the law.

The first report of the committee did not extend the judicial power to cases arising under the Constitution. But such a provision was later inserted by direct action of the Convention. Authority of such magnitude, though so logically necessary, could not have been conceded except for the confidence of the framers of the Constitution in the judicial function. Mr. William Draper Lewis has recently reviewed the conflicting opinions of historians as to the intent of the framers of the Constitution regarding the power of courts to declare acts of other departments of government void for repugnancy to the Constitution, and concludes that the great weight of evidence supports the contention that such power was intended. He says that twenty-seven members of the Convention expressed views in support of such judicial power whereas only three "may have denied its existence." But it is to be noted that the authority given, when exercised according to the intent of the Constitution, is

strictly judicial. It is to be exercised not in
the abstract, but only in the concrete; not in
reference to all possible cases, but only upon
the facts of a single case. It considers powers,
not policies. It is to be called into action only
by judicial process and affects directly only
parties to the litigation.

The Convention had given careful consideration to the proposal for a council of revi-
sion, with power to pass upon the expediency
and propriety of legislative acts. It had also
considered that the legislature might be
given the right to call upon the judges of the
Supreme Court for opinions as to the constitutionality of pending legislation. It discussed at length a motion "that the supreme
national judiciary should be associated with
the executive in the revisionary power" and
act with the President in exercising the veto.
But all these proposals were discarded. Most
of the members of the Convention thought
that the judiciary should be kept quite free
from the consideration of political policy.
Gerry said the expositors of the laws should
not be made legislators. Martin said: "A
knowledge of mankind, and of legislative affairs, cannot be presumed to belong in a

higher degree to the judges than to the legislature. And as to the constitutionality of
laws, that point will come before the judges
in their official character." Gorham thought
"that the judges ought to carry into the exposition of the laws no prepossessions with
regard to them." And Rutledge concluded
the debate with the statement that he thought
"judges, of all men, the most unfit to be concerned in the revisionary council. The judges
ought never to give their opinion on a law,
till it comes before them." He thought the
executive should seek the advice only of officers of state. It was clearly the intent of the
Convention that the tribunal which was to
pass upon the constitutionality of legislative
acts should neither possess the power, nor be
exposed to the danger, of invading the legislative province by acting upon motives of
expediency. The power given to the judiciary
was great, but it was strictly judicial.

But while the majority of the Convention
restricted the judiciary to things strictly judicial, the delegates as a whole supported
every proposal to make the judges absolutely
independent within their proper province.
Every plan submitted included tenure during

good behavior and regular compensation
which might not be reduced during a judge's
incumbency. Although many of the delegates
had had experience with the popular election
of local judges and magistrates in their respective states, yet there was no proposal to
choose federal judges by such method. Some
at first thought they should be chosen by the
Senate. But as stated, the motion for their
appointment by the President with the advice and consent of the Senate carried without dissent. The suggestion that judges be
removable by the executive on the address of
both houses of the legislature was over-
whelmingly rejected. The suggestion was
borrowed from the English system, but the
motion received the vote of but one state,
Connecticut. As Curtis says, the delegates
recognized that questions would necessarily
arise as to whether one of the departments of
government had overstepped the limits as-
signed to it as against the others, and whether
the action of the general or the state governments were within their appropriate spheres.
These constitutional questions were to be
subjected to the arbitrament of the national
judiciary, and, as Curtis says, it was almost

universally felt that this delicate and important power should be confined to judges whose tenure of office could be touched only by the solemn process of accusation and impeachment.

This was the timely fruition of man's legal evolution: a government established by the people, made subject in its basic charter to the law, and the exposition and application of the law entrusted to an independent judiciary, acting in accordance with the orderly processes of the law: a government, not of caprice or arbitrary will, but "under God and the law"—God as revealed through man's untrammeled conscience and the law as established by man's informed and disciplined reason.

Magna Charta established a court that was no longer an appanage of the king's person. It freed the law from the sovereign will. The Constitution established the judicial power on a parity with the executive power. It subjected the sovereign will to the arbitrament of the law. These were great steps toward freedom because our freedom has been established as the law has been established. We gain freedom only as we subject our lives to the law of our being. As Cicero said at the beginning of our legal evolution: "We are in bondage to the law in order that we may be free."

PART FOUR

THE SPIRIT OF THE LEGAL PROFESSION

IN RETROSPECT AND PROSPECT

XIX.

THE WAY OF THE LAW

THUS far the influence of the profession on public law has been emphasized. But it should not be overlooked that through all the years the lawyers were also administering the private law. They were constantly dealing with the law as it affected the rights and liabilities of individuals. They were the ministers of the courts and the champions of opposing litigants. They drafted pleadings, made arguments, and prepared journal entries embodying judgments of the courts. They acted as intermediaries and made compromises and settlements. They formed corporations, partnerships, and other associations. They drafted wills and contracts, settled estates, and directed guardians, receivers, and other trustees. They acted as counselors—the finest part of their professional service and the least rewarded. Counsel, like preventive medicine, is never appreciated because the client, like the patient, never realizes what evil has been forestalled. As counselors they instructed the

ignorant, directed the doubtful, guided the
wayward, comforted the afflicted, and helped
to preserve the peace. By far the greatest
part of the lawyer's work is done for individuals and private associations and is not
concerned directly with public law or state
policy. This work is not spectacular, but it is
quite essential to a well-ordered society. The
influence of a good lawyer indeed is often
more effective for the maintenance of peace
and order than the mandates of a court. Justice can frequently be effected more quickly
and less expensively by him than by cum-
brous judicial process.

It has been noted how the law developed
in Rome under the emperors and in England
under the kings. The most tyrannical rulers
concerned themselves only with state cases.
The private law was thus permitted to grow
under the direction of the profession. The
processes of the law were continually improved and the people were continuously
educated. Man's tendency to trade was the
principal incentive for the expansion of the
law. As man's business enterprise expanded,
civilization expanded. The business of the
world could be developed only under the

protection of the law. Business, like a great
ruthless tractor, moves over the earth and
breaks the incrustation of humanity; the
seeds of understanding take root in its wake;
and charity is the harvest of such understanding. Thus is the soil prepared for the growth
of the law. Men are prone to think of the
law and lawyers as dealing only with controversies. But truth and justice are not discovered in antagonisms. "Truth is lost in the
midst of disputes," said the old Latin maxim.
The greatest and best part of the lawyer's
work is the establishment of the law, and
that is done best in an atmosphere of understanding and good will.

Thus the law tentatively but patiently and
earnestly worked itself into the lives of the
great mass of men. Even while its ministers
were ruthlessly opposed by the sovereign will
in matters of state policy, they continued to
devote themselves to the establishment of the
law between man and man. Though the judgments of courts like Coke's were set at nought
in state cases, their judgments in private
causes built a firm foundation for Anglo-
American law. The way of the development
of law is illustrated by the fact that Coke,

after being deposed as judge and imprisoned in the Tower, persisted in writing his Commentaries. His writings continued to influence the course of the law long after the influence of the king was as dead as a mackerel.

The great bulk of legal work is routine and repetition. Much of a lawyer's office work is formal and most of his court work is ritualistic. Most cases are determined by precedent. As Justice Holmes said, every judge must eat a lot of sawdust. And every practicing lawyer must suffer the monotony of the daily grind.

But the purpose of the law is to meet humanity's needs and those needs are continually changing. Ever and anon the law is confronted with new conditions. The members of the profession are men, and the best of them are men of broad sympathies and therefore very susceptible to the aims and aspirations of their fellows. While they daily minister to man's petty needs, they also plan a better course. Though their education and experience are of the past, their influence is on the present and the future.

They are conservative because they must base their opinion as to what can be done upon their knowledge of what has been done. But they are also insurgents because they must break the barriers that bar the way to things that must be done. Bearing the armory of the past they "beat upon the walls of ancient categories." They are constant champions of right and opponents of wrong, but they find that man's ideas of right and wrong change from age to age. They are therefore frequently called upon, as Justice Cardozo said, to make a choice so nicely balanced that a new right and a new wrong are produced. By counsel and contract, by legislation and decision, the profession continually establishes new precedents as the law of man's being is discovered and revealed. The way of the law is like the way of a man rowing a boat: while he moves forward he looks back; though buffeted by current, wind, and wave, he keeps his bark in alignment with past points while he propels it steadily toward a point ahead.

The principal work of the profession is to assess ancient customs in terms of future values, to protect those which have enduring worth, and carefully and slowly change those which no longer suit the conditions. Its aim is not merely to follow ancient precedent, but to discover the principle that prompted the precedent. The law has in it both an element of stability and an element of change. The law is not a dead letter, but the living word. The law is the wine of life; it is not merely the bottle that contains it. The plodding experience of mankind treads out the juice of the grape, and the spirit of the law is the ferment that transforms and preserves it for future use.

XX.

WORK OF THE PROFESSION

AFTER the ratification of the Constitution, the character of professional service changed, but the need for able lawyers and judges still continued. The changed condition of political and social affairs gave rise to novel questions, requiring the sharpest perspicuity. Cases arose for which there were no precedents in the common law of England. Analytical reason, working upon experience of the past and scientific understanding of the problems, had to supply controlling principles. Controversies had to be settled by an innate sense of right, in the spirit of justice. The service of the profession during the interpretative period was as noteworthy, if not so noted, as its service during the formative period of our national history.

The beginning of our government was so auspicious that we are prone to think that its success was assured. Because of its full-blown birth we assume its full-grown strength. But from the beginning it was assailed by dangerous forces without and within. Its most ardent champions professed the gravest doubts. Only the ignorant were arrogant. Such arrogance indeed was one of the great obstacles to the principal saving agency. The hostility to law and lawyers which had existed in colonial times continued in certain classes after the Revolution. This opposition, when supported by the general swing toward unrestricted democracy, prompted a very definite attempt to give the untrained and incompetent ready access to the bar and the bench. The effect was injurious because it weakened the very fiber of the profession. The bench and bar were then criticized for faults which the critics had caused.

In spite of such opposition, however, the

lawyers continued to lead in public affairs. Such leadership was maintained not through any definite conscious effort for leadership, but through unselfish devotion to professional traditions. The Anglo-Saxon doctrine of supremacy of law was maintained through constructive juristic activity. The respect of English-speaking peoples for law and order has frequently been remarked. Their patient adherence to constituted authority under conditions which lead to revolution in other countries has often been noted. Such adherence is not due to an abject submission on the part of the people, but to the fact that the law has generally been made worthy of their respect. Order has not been maintained by arbitrary will and intimidating force, but by the adjustment of rules, principles, and standards so that the law could expand to meet man's ideas of natural right and inherent justice, and square with his sense of sound reason and practical utility. The influence of the profession continued to work in two ways. While it continually adjusted the law to man's growing needs, it also continuously expanded man's understanding of the need of the law.

Where the need of the profession was so great, the professional influence had to be increased and expanded. That this requirement has been met is evidenced by the fact that there is a higher ratio of lawyers to total population in this country than in any other. In order that the quality of professional service should not fail, legal education was made available and the ancient standards of education maintained. Quite early in the history of the country the need was felt for a more formal course of study than the ordinary law office afforded. Following the lead of William and Mary College, Columbia College in 1793 established a professorship of law and James Kent was made the first incumbent, his later lectures being published as Kent's Commentaries. A law school was established at Harvard in 1817, at Yale in 1824, in Virginia in 1826, and at the University of Cincinnati in 1833. Thereafter the growth of law schools increased rapidly as state universities were established. Such law schools have produced teachers of the highest order. Langdell of Harvard, Minor of Virginia, Cooley of Michigan—to mention but one from a section of the country—were teachers of broad understanding and writers of professional skill. Their standards have been maintained and the scope of their work expanded by worthy successors. Such men as Pound, Stone and Wigmore, Mechem and Hall exemplify their work in our time.

But in spite of the generality and excellence of legal education, an increasing need was felt for some agency which could preserve the unity of the profession throughout the different states and maintain its standards and traditions in practice. In 1878 the American Bar Association was organized. While it has never been able to draw into its membership a majority of all lawyers, it has always commanded the active support of most of the leaders of the profession. Its influence has therefore been great. It has been able to voice the best legal opinion. In spite of the fact that the ablest lawyers have generally represented clients of great property and extensive business and, through their very loyalty to clients, have tended to overemphasize the importance of property rights and "business interests," and in spite of the tendency of many lawyers to technical legalistic thinking, still their concerted influence has generally served human needs. The Association has done for the profession in America, at least in part, what the Inns of Court have done in England. It has championed high standards of legal education and strict requirements for admission to the bar. It formulated and published the *Canons of Legal Ethics*. Through them and by more direct discipline it has exerted a strong influence for true professional conduct. It has constantly studied the operation and effect of laws and has brought about many amendments of law and improvements in its administration. It has been a guardian of the established principles of Anglo-Saxon jurisprudence and again and again has championed the judiciary when its very position of independence precluded the judges from speaking in their own defense. Unlike the ordinary trade association or union, it has not made its own interests or the income of its members its object. It has set a constant example of devotion to public service. With the help of the State, County, and City Bar Associations which it has inspired and encouraged, it has given direction and force to that professional influence which society has found so essential to its welfare.

XXI.

INDUSTRIALISM AND DEMOCRACY

IT has not always been easy to maintain the professional influence. During the industrial revolution and the heyday of democracy the spirit of the profession became weak and public indifference to it grew strong. Our great material development came at the general cost of things spiritual and professional. As Dr. Alexis Carrel says, "We have applied to man concepts belonging to the mechanical world. We have neglected thought, moral suffering, sacrifice, beauty, and peace. We have treated the individual as a chemical substance, a machine, or a part of a machine. We have amputated his moral, esthetic, and religious functions." Our scientific and commercial advance was due to the fact that the attention and emphasis of life were upon material rather than spiritual values. And one of the evil results was that the profession suffered another Iron Age. The legal profession, like all professions that deal with the imponderables of life, suffered a subsidence of its ideals. Man's crass materialism made him a victim of his avarice, and the old world had to learn again that cupidity corrodes and corrupts.

The industrial revolution took a far swing in America. The liberty to live became a license to possess. Political freedom became industrial indulgence. The industrialism of the North overcame the agrarianism of the South and the commercialism of the East swept over the West like a prairie fire. Influences which might have been expected to restrain seemed only to increase the tendency. The Puritans, the Quakers, the Mennonites, in their zeal to withstand the blandishments of life suppressed even the embellishments, and the energy of life was spent in practical pursuits. The result was that prudence and thrift were overemphasized. The higher professions do not thrive on thrift.

An undeveloped country made men drunk with desire for wealth. The pioneers exploited the reserves of nature and their successors exploited the reserves of human nature. The glamour of gain blinded men to the reality of unseen things. The whole materialistic mirage misled men into vain pursuits, and not until the forces of life were spent did they realize the futility of the things they sought. Their cunning made them cruel. Rugged individualism became a mere shield for intense and bitter selfishness; it made man unsocial and uncivil. Businessmen prided themselves on their relentlessness to competitors and their indifference to the public weal. They affected a high disdain for politics. They boasted of their greater concern for good business than good government. Their indifference blinded them to the fact that there can be no good business without good government, and bitter experience was the price of their blind indifference.

Although in some respects industrialism and democracy were opposed to each other, in other respects they accentuated each other. The tendency of industrialism to create a plutocracy brought about extreme assertions of democracy. The selfishness of the classes produced the self-assertion of the masses. Selfishness always begets selfishness. Class consciousness begets bitterness. Then the work of the instigator is rife.

The exploitation of business by the barons was followed by the exploitation of democracy by the demagogues. Public offices became political plums—they were distributed freely, rather than discharged faithfully. Office was not looked upon as an opportunity for service, but as the incumbent's turn for self-aggrandizement. Government was not considered so much the public's business as a public game. Personal and party rivalry prevailed, and retaliation was indulged at the cost of civil service. Even education cultivated the feeling of rivalry, and the youth were trained to prevail in the game of life rather than to persevere in the right way of life. All the forces of life, in both private and public business, were geared to getting instead of giving. The inordinate greed of some seemed to make it necessary for all to be greedy. Most men thought they had to be lustful to live. Personal gain was the goal, with no thought for the common sources of life. Patriotism prevailed only under the fear of some foreign foe, and the devotion to the cause of any part of humanity was dependent on organized hatred of some other part of humanity.

Rackets and strikes, depressions and wars were the natural crop of such conduct. The evils persisted because men persisted in being emotional and wilful instead of reasonable and lawful. Men continued to be the victims of greed, deceit, and arbitrary force because they failed to establish and maintain the law in conformity to their nature as rational beings. Where such lawlessness prevailed there was small room for the professional spirit. It is no wonder therefore that many lawyers forgot their high calling and beguiled their lives by seeking wealth and tinsel titles.

The general tendency of such a way of life in America was to undermine the balance of our republican institutions. Whether the trend to more popular but less efficient forms of government was democracy's reaction to industrialism or merely the inherent tendency of republics to be influenced by centrifugal instead of centripetal forces, cannot be definitely asserted. But certain it is that the general direction of our movement has been away from that unity of forces which the Constitution ordained. First the party movement destroyed the purpose of the electoral college and subjected the executive to popular vote. The direct election of Senators brought the upper house of Congress under popular control, and thereby removed one of the principal reasons for a bicameral legislature. In numerous ways the popular influence has been made more direct, with the consequence that too often those who should lead up have had to play down. Only by most diligent effort, supplied mainly by the legal profession, has the independence of the United States judiciary been preserved.

Departing from the fine example of the federal Constitution, the great majority of the separate states provided in their constitutions that judges should be elected by the people for short terms only. This was a retrograde movement and has produced only evil results. It has insidiously and persistently lowered the quality of judicial service. It was prompted by a misconception of the purpose of the judicial function, and was carried into effect by the general tendency to subject every public office to the popular will. It is well to allow the popular will free play upon the legislative function, but the whole course of history teaches that the judiciary has functioned best when free from the arbitrary will of either crown or commons. The imperative idea stagnates legal development and thwarts the course of justice.

Rufus Choate, in his famous speech in the Massachusetts State Convention of 1853, while discussing the question of how to get and keep the best judge, defined his ideal as follows:

In the first place, he should be profoundly learned in all the learning of the law, and he must know how to use that learning. Will any one stand up here to deny this? In this day, boastful, glorious for its advancing popular, professional, scientific, and all education, will any one disgrace himself by doubting the necessity of deep and continued studies, and various and thorough attainments, to the bench? He is to know, not merely the law which you make, and the legislature makes, not constitutional and statute law alone, but that other ampler, that boundless jurisprudence, the common law, which the successive generations of the State have silently built up; that old code of freedom which we brought with us in the Mayflower and Arabella, but which in the progress of centuries we have ameliorated and enriched, and adapted wisely to the necessities of a busy, prosperous, and wealthy community,—that he must know. And where to find it? In volumes which you must count by hundreds, by thousands; filling libraries; exacting long labors, —the labors of a life-time, abstracted from business, from politics; but assisted by taking part in an active judicial administration; such labors as produced the wisdom and won the fame of Parsons and Marshall, and Kent and Story, and Holt and Mansfield. If your system of appointment and tenure does not present a motive, a help for such labors and such learning; if it discourages, if it disparages them, in so far it is a failure.

In the next place, he must be a man, not merely upright, not merely honest and well-intentioned,— this of course,—but a man who will not respect persons in judgment. And does not every one here agree to this also? Dismissing, for a moment, all theories about the mode of appointing him, or the time for which he shall hold office, sure I am, we all demand,. that as far as human virtue, assisted by the best contrivances of human wisdom, can attain to it, he shall not respect persons in judgment. He shall know nothing about the parties, everything about the case. He shall do everything for justice; nothing for himself; nothing for his friend; nothing for his patron; nothing for his sovereign.

If on one side is the executive power and the legislature and the people,—the sources of his honors,
the givers of his daily bread,—and on the other an
individual nameless and odious, his eye is to see
neither, great nor small; attending only to the
"trepidations of the balance." If a law is passed by
an unanimous legislature, clamored for by the general voice of the public, and a cause is before him
on it, in which the whole community is on one side
and an individual nameless or odious on the other,
and he believes it to be against the Constitution, he
must so declare it,—or there is no judge. If Athens
comes there to demand that the cup of hemlock be
put to the lips of the wisest of men; and he believes
that he has not *corrupted the youth, nor omitted to
worship the gods of the city, nor introduced new
divinities of his own*, he must deliver him, although
the thunder light on the unterrified brow.

The outstanding purpose of courts in our
system of government is to give security to
justice against power. They are the last guard
against that worst form of tyranny, the tyranny of the majority. They are society's last
stand for reason against emotion, for order
against force. When their independence is
lost their efficiency is lost. Judges dominated
by fear of the populace have proved as ineffi-
cient and as despicable as judges dominated
by fear of the king.

The deterioration of the character of our state courts contributed to the subsidence of the professional spirit generally. The influence of the judicial office is great; the incumbent should be a pattern of professional propriety. When the judge is a man of common principles the practice in his court degenerates to a low level. The demoralizing effect of the commercial and popular influences was so great that the true standards of the profession were lost. The practice of the law descended to the level of the practices of trade and politics. Even the schools, with few exceptions, were content to make robots proficient in the practice, rather than to imbue lawyers with the spirit of their calling.

As the commercialization of our country, with its inordinate desire for profit, destroyed all pride of production, and changed a country of patriots into a nation of traders; so the democratic movement, with its inordinate desire for popularity, tended to destroy the ideal of the law and convert a profession of lawyers into a guild of legal hucksters and political mountebanks. The general standards of success in life became proficiency in the scramble for possessions and proficiency

in the scramble for political power. Hilaire
Belloc has drafted an unanswerable indictment of commercialism. He says:

First, the Commercial Spirit tends to make wealth
the test of excellence. . . . All men feel wealth to
be an attribute, but, under the Commercial Spirit,
wealth becomes a quality: it is regarded as Courage, Beauty or Strength are regarded elsewhere.
. . . So antagonistic are the spirits of Commerce
and Husbandry that the preponderance of the one
endangers the very life of the other. [Two conse-
quences are] the universal prevalence of gambling,
from the betting on horse and dog racing by the
population as a whole to the ceaseless speculation
in shares and currency among the richer half of
the community;—. . . the sale of honours, policies
and contracts, the bribery and blackmailing of individual politicians, the degradation of the Press,
and all the rest of the nasty business.

And Dr. Alexis Carrel has dissected the error
of the democratic dogma. Dr. Carrel says:
"As it was impossible to raise the inferior
types, the only means of producing democratic equality among men was to bring all to
the lowest level. Thus vanished personality."
And the professional spirit almost vanished
with it.

XXII.

THE REMNANT

WE might apply to our professional history the words of Isaiah to Judah: "Except the Lord of hosts had left unto us a very small remnant, we should have been as Sodom, and we should have been like unto Gomorrah." But always there was the modicum, the remnant of the faithful. These were inspired by a few devoted teachers, and they found justification and defense in the judiciary of the United States and of those few states that still maintained the independence of their courts. In America as in England, judges of secure tenure have exemplified the spirit of the legal profession. They have proved that there is in man a sense of justice which in fair circumstances may be trusted. While at times their conservative attitude toward the established economic order has led them into unwarranted opposition to new laws, their decisions as a whole have been more progressive, more in sympathy with movements for the common welfare than those of the judges elected for short terms.

Contrary to the expectations and representations of those who championed popular courts, the work of such courts has been reactionary. It demonstrates again that the law cannot develop naturally, it cannot grow with man's growth, under intimidated and obsequious judges.

Under the aegis of the courts of character that remained, the remnant of true lawyers continued their practice according to professional principles. They withstood the surge of the money-mad mob and patiently bore what Daniel Webster said was the lawyer's lot—to work hard, live well, and die poor. They eschewed the practices of the political tricksters and set an example of honorable dealing. They, together with the faithful few of the other professions, were able to maintain some semblance of a genteel element in society. They did not, to borrow the expression of Dr. Carrel, "develop an elite"; but they did maintain some values in life above the standards of the industrialists and egalitarians.

Nearly every local community had at least one real lawyer. He was always an influence in civic affairs. Generally he was the princi-

pal spokesman of the community. Although
it was neither proclaimed nor acknowledged,
a paternal feeling for his people was in his
heart. He opposed their mistakes and defended them against imposition. He championed and supported every movement for
improvement of public affairs. Being informed, however, as to past efforts and
learned in established principles, he frequently felt called upon to oppose the nos-
trums of would-be reformers. He was therefore considered a reactionary. This was of
course unjust, for anyone who fights for an
ideal, even though his ideal seems to lie in
the past, is driving the world on to the future. The real reactionary is the man who is
satisfied with the present. The true lawyer is
marked with divine dissatisfaction. He is
therefore sympathetic with all human aspirations for improvement of the ways of life. In
all his contacts with life, it is as natural for
him to strive for justice and righteousness as
it is for the tendrils of a plant to reach out
for sustenance and light.

It is the very nature of the spirit of the legal profession to make one feel a personal responsibility for the administration of justice.

A lawyer imbued with such spirit is never lost in his own concerns or the concerns of his clients. It lifts him above the wish to win and makes him a champion of truth. It raises him above the specific suit to a consideration of the general principle embracing all similar suits. It elevates his view above the particular case and makes him conscious of the system by which such particular cases are determined. He is therefore continually interested in the work of improving the administration of the law and the means of maintaining order.

Since the law bears upon all human relations and endeavors, those who practice it are brought into contact with all kinds of men. The lawyer therefore grows to be all things to all men. "To know all is to forgive all," so the lawyer develops a broad charity. He has none of the severity of the puritan or the narrowness of the prude. The breadth of his judgment and sympathy gives him a strong influence. The weight of his influence is keenly felt by those who oppose the things he champions and by those who champion the things he opposes. Frequently, therefore, he is bitterly assailed. He is maligned and ridiculed and misrepresented. But the true lawyer bears these things with equanimity. He takes them as a part of the burden of his calling. He is not so anxious to win men's favor as he is to be worthy of their respect.

So in spite of all obstacles, including the default of many of their brethren of the bar, the remnant of the faithful maintained the professional spirit. In spite of the self-seeking of politicians, they did not lust for power; in spite of the greed of industrialists, they did not become the victims of avarice. With gracious generosity they stood by and allowed the fruits of their own wisdom and effort to be garnered by ungrateful clients. They served the rich and the poor, the high and the low, with true professional indifference to class or caste. Without fanfare or parade, with little concerted effort and no "drives," mindful of the shortness of life and the futility of most human effort, they patiently adhered to the service of the law and the best traditions of their calling. With patience and perseverance they sought and studied the law; by precept and example they taught and practiced the law; and to the best of their ability they maintained the objects of the law, justice and order.

One who endeavors and endures for justice and righteousness is sustained by unexpected, unseen, and unknown forces. His consciousness of right doing is a source of strength; his humble sacrifice becomes a source of exaltation. Other men who see his heroic struggle are compelled by the moral force of their own nature, that part of them which is divine, to support his cause. It was due to this truth that the remnant was able to keep alive the spirit of the legal profession. And so we can say as Paul said in his letter to the Romans: "Even so then at this present time also there is a remnant according to the election of grace."

XXIII.

THE PROFESSIONAL SPIRIT

THE legal profession was the first profession. The priesthood was of course older, but it was not professional. It was a hereditary class or social caste; its service was mystical, Levitical, or ritualistic, and its influence

strictly sacerdotal. At the time of the formation of the legal profession in Rome, the
practice of medicine was almost exclusively
the work of Greek slaves. The Greeks had
taken the first steps to elevate the art of heal-
ing from sorcery to a science and the Romans
had erected near the temple of Aesculapius
something like a hospital, but still the work
was largely domestic in character and there
was neither professional feeling nor standards of practice among the physicians and
surgeons. The professional attitude came
later to the men of medicine and the men of
the church. The early teachers were quite in-
dividualistic. The teaching profession and
the engineering profession have been developed in quite modern times. It cannot yet
be said that the men of the press and of
banking have developed professions. As the
lawyers have been, so they continue to be
pioneers in the establishment and extension
of professional principles. They should lead
in demonstrating the value of the professional attitude to the commonweal.

The increase of professions and the extension of the professional attitude will fill society's inherent need for standards and prin-

ciples of life, will provide more adequately
those benefits which have heretofore been
supplied by an aristocracy, elite, or nobility,
but without the evils which attend those arbitrary classes and castes. Humanity has a
constant need for a secondary system of laws,
a code of decorum and taste which cannot be
crystallized into legislation or enforced by
judicial decree. The observance of such a
code is voluntary. It is inculcated by example. It is binding only upon those who feel
it. But it is an essential element in social evolution.

The great evil of uncontrolled democracy
is that it thwarts that process of social improvement. Democracy tends toward ochloc-
racy because it refuses to recognize the
leaders that nature produces. Men of truth
and character are too stern for it. It does not
distinguish between service and servility. It
is a weak sovereign, too susceptible to flat-
tery. It seeks its kind and brings all to its
level. Even men who know better play down
to it and justify their subserviency on the
grounds of expediency. James Madison referred to this influence as the great *vortex*—

the tendency of the popular element to submerge all other elements.

The great republics have made attempts to establish a balance between the democratic and aristocratic elements. But they have not succeeded—not permanently. The balance could not be maintained. The true patriots have been powerless both against the selfish action of the arbitrary classes and against the destructive reaction of the undiscriminating masses.

Moreover the democratic element can operate successfully only within a limited area. It has done well only in the city-state and the town meeting. This is caused by a natural limitation of the human intellect. Man can know well only those whom he knows intimately, and it is impossible to know men intimately over large areas and in large numbers. In spite of the developments of the press, the radio, and the cinema, there are still mechanical limitations upon popular government. The makers of the Constitution attempted to overcome this difficulty by establishing a representative republic. They provided for a succession of selections by limited numbers. Madison referred to this process as *filtration*. But in spite of his forewarning the process has been weakened by the insidious influence of the popular *vortex*.

Now if the down-pull of government by plebiscite is to be arrested, if the vortex movement of democracy is to be counterbalanced, it will be accomplished mainly by the grace of the professional spirit. The professions afford the most practical method available today. They are established and have proved their worth. They have demonstrated that men can, while observing the highest standards of a professional code, still live useful and glorious lives, happy lives, lives that are successful in the truest sense of the word.

The professional spirit sets its seal against self-seeking and self-aggrandizement. It awakens a social consciousness and conscience. It tends to inspire men with the zeal of the scientist, the devotion of the saint. It teaches that by the advancement of men wise and good all men prosper. It makes ridiculous those designing individuals who obtrude themselves into places which they do not merit and cannot grace. The professions are founded upon merit. They impose standards of admission and standards of practice. A position in a profession must be earned. It cannot be inherited as a place in an aristocracy or plutocracy. But the professions are open to all who will submit to their discipline.

Above all, the professions afford a selective process by which the best may be chosen for the service of society in accordance with the natural order of social evolution. Each calling knows its own best men. The legal profession should have a greater influence in the selection of judges; the medical profession in the selection of public health officers. There is more reason to classify society by trades and professions than by arbitrary geographic divisions. Arbitrary boundaries have less and less justification as the facilities of travel and communication increase. Government should follow the practice of society generally by encouraging the development of specialties. It should then look to its specialists for best service.

To get the maximum benefit from the professional spirit its influence must be extended to all vocations. There is no worth-while work that cannot have its *esprit de corps* and a consciousness of its obligations to society. Advanced positions along this line have been established by pioneers in the law. Outposts of the movement have already made satisfactory contact with the labor problem. Dean Lloyd Garrison, writing about the Wisconsin Labor Relations Act, points out that if a complaint is made that an employer is engaged in practices affecting employees which are not consistent with practices of employers enjoying satisfactory relations with labor organizations, the complaint must be referred to the employers' committee; and if a complaint is made that a labor organization is engaged in practices affecting employers which are not consistent with practices of labor organizations enjoying satisfactory relations with employers, the complaint must be referred to the labor committee. He then says:

These provisions are, so far as I know, an entirely new departure in labor legislation. They proceed on the theory that industry and organized labor, if given responsibility to maintain standards within their own ranks, will respond and will accomplish more than the state alone could do by compulsion. . . . The fact that leaders of the organized labor movement in Wisconsin accepted the measure and were willing to have the state aid them in maintaining proper standards of union conduct is the best sign that the experiment will work.

What may be accomplished in very practical affairs by men actuated by a fine professional spirit and a sense of responsibility to the public is illustrated by the record of the Corps of Engineers of the United States Army. Construction works of the greatest magnitude, involving billions of dollars, have been completed under their direction without fraud or suspicion of corruption. Their performance is a refutation of the statement that the profit motive is an essential part of man's incentive to work. Men of assured position and respectable income have surmounted avarice and rendered service of inestimable value.

Thomas Jefferson based his high hope for democracy upon general education, but experience teaches that general education needs some means of continuing discipline, some medium for the inspiration which comes from concerted effort and devotion to a calling. If the blessings of popular government are not to be lost, if the forces of democracy are to be kept in balance with the forces of evolution, men in general will have to be motivated by something like the professional spirit that has moved and sustained the great men of the law.

XXIV.

IN CONCLUSION

THAT we are experiencing some fundamental economic changes is generally conceded. That we are at the end of an epoch, that a new era is at hand, has been frequently remarked. What these changes signify, what the new social order will be, no one is able to tell. But the legal profession now as ever will have to lead in adjusting the law to the new conditions. It will have to discover and formulate the principles underlying the changes. Laws and a system of administration which meet the prevailing sense of social justice will have to be provided.

The function of the law and courts of justice in the body politic is largely the extension of the function of reason and conscience in the individual. The individual in the light of reason and conscience interprets his experience into principles of conduct. He determines what it is right and best to do and then, if he is a person of character, he adheres to those principles against the urge of emotion and passion. So the body politic brings its reason to bear upon its problems mainly through the legislative function and then, if it has courts of character, the principles which its reason and conscience dictate are maintained against the assertion of arbitrary will and force. As a man develops and changes his interests and occupations in life, he must make corresponding adjustment in his principles of conduct. So the state as it changes its mode of life, as it shifts its aims and purposes with changing times and conditions, must modify its rules of civil conduct. The methods by which such rules of conduct are enforced must also from time to time be changed to meet man's changing notions of what is just and fair and expeditious.

The spirit of our legal institutions which has brought us thus far in our progress will meet our present needs. That spirit which delivered the law from mystery and superstition and established the Twelve Tables in the public Forum, which wrested its adminis-

tration from the pontifical caste and gave it
to public officers, which broke the rigidity of
formulary practice and superimposed the jurisdiction of equity on the strict letter of the
law, which rescued the rule of reason from
Anglo-Saxon customs and substituted the
judgment of twelve honest men for the
chance of ordeal, the right of conscience for
the might of battle, which divorced the courts
from the king's person and substituted due
process for the king's prerogative, which established a new government upon a written
Constitution which gave security to justice
against power—the spirit which has done
these things and has taught men generally to
understand the virtue and the value of the
law, if we trust it, still will prove sufficient
for our every exigency.

The law must be thought of more as we
think of the law of physics or the law of
chemistry, not as mere naked command but
as a social phenomenon. We must seek it with
an open mind. We must patiently strive to
understand it. We should not be so arbitrary
about it. Neither the arbitrary will of the
people nor the arbitrary will of a dictator
can prevail against the fundamental prin-

ciples of our evolution. The well-springs of life will surge forth in spite of judicial decree or general plebiscite. Our bitter partisanship and pride of opinion are of no avail; they serve only to confuse and confound us. As the true law is discovered and declared it proves beneficent to all. Differences of opinion as to the right way are bound to occur, and experimentation is at times our only course. But destructive opposition can never help us on the way to our common goal.

We should not be too attached to the shibboleths of past periods. Words and phrases like "peace," "order," "liberty," "freedom and equality," "democracy," "neutrality," "security," "self-government," and "local rule" express the aspiration of an age and are apt to confuse the thinking of succeeding ages. The true criterion of one era is apt to become a deception in another. The demagogues and mountebanks soon learn the aspirates and then they unctuously mouth the shibboleths in order that they may "go over." Too many campaigns have been won by slogans instead of sense. Not words but works are the true test. Glittering terms of general meaning are no doubt necessary for the expression of our hopes, but our present need is always the law.

The world cries for peace but world war is imminent. All the sentimentalizing of the peace societies and all the resolves of the pacifists are in themselves of no avail. Sentimental thinking serves only to beguile us in our errors, and unqualified resolutions not to fight are abject surrenders to the evil of life. The goddess of justice would be not only blind but also impotent if disarmed. Peace, like liberty, can be realized only by sacrifice. Nations, like men, can maintain peace only by uniting their efforts and risking their lives against those who disturb it. We may have our selfishness and our narrow nationalism, our greed for gain and our pride of power, and *war*—or, by eschewing those things, we may establish the means for the maintenance of justice and have *peace*. Peace comes like freedom, to the extent that it is possible for it to come, only in the wake of the law.

The spirit of the legal profession will in time establish institutions under which men and peoples may live and grow with the maximum of freedom, institutions to which the industrial and labor organizations will defer and to which the nations themselves will submit their differences with abiding faith in the reasonableness and good conscience of disinterested men. The professional spirit can supply such men. That principle of social growth which made the slave a freeman, the serf a freeholder, the subject a free citizen, will not now abandon the people of the world to industrial bondage or any form of absolutism. Man will mold his economic as he has molded his political fate. That social evolution which expanded the family into a clan, the clan into a country, feudal tenures into sovereign states, and superimposed upon sovereign states a permanent federal government, plenary in power but restricted to rule of law—that evolution will not stop short of a world arrangement under which the nations of the world, like the men of the nations, may develop and express their individualities subject to the commonweal according to the law of life.

That we cannot have the millennium at once should not discourage us from maintaining it as our goal. Though we cannot arrive at the goal we still may advance in that direction. No matter how futile our individual efforts or the efforts of our age may seem, still, looking back through all the ages, we can discern a line of progress, and we know that all improvement has come through the effort of those who, in spite of failure, have continued to try. The motion of our evolution seems wavelike; there are periods of progression and periods of regression. Even if we are caught in a retrograde movement, even if, as some are fond of predicting, our civilization is doomed to a slump, still we may rest assured that it will make a difference to succeeding generations which way we are facing when we go down.

The men who have been able to transcend their times and make their lives an inspiration to succeeding ages are the men who have obtained their support from the unseen things which are eternal. The great lawyers of all times, though not always orthodox, have been men of deep religious sensibilities. Cicero's philosophy was almost on a plane with the religious teachings of the church fathers who followed him so closely in Rome. The moral courage and the insight of men like Coke and Blackstone were prompted by an abiding religious faith. Marshall's reverence for religion is well known. Men who can conceive the law must be mindful of the moral forces of life. Men who contemplate the law are naturally prompted to believe in a moral purpose of life. Paraphrasing the statement of the mystic regarding God, we may say that he who observes the word of the law is led to a belief in the law. Lawfulness becomes a source of spiritual clear-sightedness.

The men who give their lives to temporal things are mere children of their age. They are absorbed in the things that are seen and are frustrated by the affairs of their time. Being time-servers they have no time for things eternal. They learn to doubt the mythology of religion and then question the moral worth of religion. They discover that the allegories of religion are not historically true, and they then conclude that they are absolved from all religious restraints. They are actuated only by the hope of immediate gain and personal gratification. They give themselves to the lusts of the world and their spiritual forces are submerged in selfishness. But the aim of the great lawyer, like the law he espouses, is justice; and justice is essentially unselfish since it considers the inter-

ests of all men. The man of the law has a
sense of the ultimate, a deep conviction of
the moral order of the universe, and, as Justice Holmes has said, his thought finds unity
with the infinite. The spirit of the legal
profession is in harmony with all things
spiritual.

The basic concepts of the law, indeed the
sources of our legal evolution, are founded in
religion. "Human dignity," "the equality of
men before the law," "that man is sacred to
man," these and other fundamental convictions which have influenced our development
sprang from the idea of a direct relationship
between man and a supreme god. The
brotherhood of men and our most precious
rights and solemn obligations flow from that
God-man relationship and the idea that
something in man is divine.

From such general ideas and from crude
beginnings the law as we have it today has
been developed by the patient efforts and heroic sacrifices of men imbued with the spirit
of the legal profession. In so far as work in
a field so broad can be exclusive, that work
has been the labor of lawyers. The credit for
the accomplishments, whatever they are,

must go mainly to the legal profession. If from that source we have gained what we have, it is to that source that we must look for future gains. If the world is to continue to have men who, in the words of Justice Holmes, can live greatly in the law, drink the bitter cup of heroism, and wear their hearts out after the unattainable, we must preserve the means of charging men with the spirit of the profession. Mainly we must rely on the schools. But the schools must be more intimately supported by the leaders of the profession. That spirit is transmitted, now as always, by association. It cannot be taught like the rule in Shelley's case, or the definition of murder. It is too great and too vital for definition. We cannot tell exactly how it passes or whom it favors. It is nothing to be dogmatic about. It eludes too definite effort. Being spirit, it moves in spiritual ways. The best way to gain it is to admire it, for what we admire we unconsciously emulate.

AUTHORITIES

PART I

MAINE, HENRY SUMNER, *Ancient Law* (3d Am. ed., from 5th London ed.), introd. and chaps. i and ii.

HOLLAND, THOMAS ERSKINE, *Elements of Jurisprudence* (7th ed.), chap. i.

MORRIS, M. F., *History of the Development of Law*.

ZANE, JOHN MAXCY, *The Story of Law*, chap. ix.

SOHM, RUDOLPH, *The Institutes* (2d ed.), Pt. I, chap. ii.

HUNTER, W. A., *Roman Law* (2d ed.), introductory and chap. iii.

BUCKLAND, W. W. and McNAIR, ARNOLD D., *Roman Law and Common Law*, chap. i.

MOORE, FRANK GARDNER, *The Roman's World*, chap. x, "The Law," pp. 305–314.

The Cambridge Ancient History, Vol. IX

ZULUETA, F. DE, "The Development of Law under the Republic," chap. xxi.

SIKES, E. E., "Literature in the Age of Cicero," chap. xviii.

Letters of Cicero, XLII (Fam. VII. 12), XXXVII (Fam. VII. 5), LXXXIII (Fam. IV. 5).

PART II

POUND, ROSCOE, *The Spirit of the Common Law*, chaps. i, ii, iii, iv.

MONTESQUIEU, C. L., *The Spirit of Laws*, Vol. I, Bk. XI, chap. vi.

Select Essays in Anglo-American Legal History,
Vol. I

  MAITLAND, FREDERIC WILLIAM, "A Prologue to
  a History of English Law," Pt. I, chap. i.

  JENKS, EDWARD, "The Development of Teutonic
  Law," Pt. I, chap. ii.

  POLLOCK, SIR FREDERICK, "English Law before
  the Norman Conquest," Pt. I, chap. iii.

  GREEN, ALICE STOPFORD, "The Centralization of
  Norman Justice under Henry II," Pt. II,
  chap. iv.

  JENKS, EDWARD, "Edward I, the English Justinian," Pt. II, chap. v.

  ZANE, JOHN MAXCY, "The Five Ages of the
  Bench and Bar of England," Pt. V, chap. xix.

BARTON, SIR D. PLUNKET, BENHAM, CHARLES, and
WATT, SIR FRANCIS, *The Story of the Inns of
Court.*

CHAMBERS, R. W., *Thomas More*, pp. 301, 316,
342.

JOHN, LORD CAMPBELL, *The Lives of the Chief
Justices of England*, Vol. I, chaps. vii, viii, ix;
Vol. II, chap. x.

ZANE, JOHN MAXCY, *The Story of Law*, chaps. xii,
xiii.

PART III

CHANNING, EDWARD, *A Student's History of the
United States*, chaps. iv, v, vi.

Select Essays in Anglo-American Legal History,
Vol. I

  REINSCH, PAUL SAMUEL, "English Common
  Law in the Early American Colonies," Pt. III,
  chap. xi.

Fiske, John, *The Critical Period of American History*, chaps. v, vi.

Elliot's Debates on the Federal Constitution (2d ed.), Vol. I; also Vol. V, "The Madison Papers," pp. 109–122, 344–351.

Bancroft, George, *History of the Constitution of the United States*, Bk. I, chaps. i and ii, pp. 5–35; Bk. III, chap. i, pp. 207–230, and chap. x, pp. 348–356.

Curtis, George Ticknor, *History of the Constitution of the United States*, Vol. I, Bk. III, chap. xiv; Vol. II, Bk. IV, chap. iii and note.

The Federalist (Henry Cabot Lodge, ed.), No. XLVII, No. XLVIII, No. LXXVIII, No. LXXIX and No. LXXX.

Lewis, William Draper, *Interpreting the Constitution*, chaps. ii, iii and notes p. 89.

Zane, John Maxcy, *The Story of Law*, chap. xv.

PART IV

Cardozo, Benjamin N., *The Growth of the Law*.

Cardozo, Benjamin N., *The Nature of the Judicial Process*.

Cardozo, Benjamin N., *Paradoxes of Legal Science*.

Zane, John Maxcy, *The Story of Law*, chap. i; also p. 287.

Pound, Roscoe, *The Spirit of the Common Law*, chaps. v and viii.

Montesquieu, C. L., *The Spirit of Laws*, Vol. II, Bk. XXI.

Select Essays in Anglo-American Legal History, Vol. I

Scrutton, Thomas Edward, "Roman Law Influence in Chancery, Church Courts, Admiralty, and Law Merchant," Pt. II, chap. vii, p. 237.

HOLDSWORTH, WILLIAM SEARLE, "The Development of the Law Merchant and Its Courts," Pt. II, chap. ix, p. 299.

BELLOC, HILAIRE, *Nature of Contemporary England*, p. 59 *et seq.*

CARREL, ALEXIS, *Man, the Unknown*, chap. vii.

LUMMUS, HENRY T., *The Trial Judge.*

BROWN, SAMUEL GILMAN, *The Life and Writings of Rufus Choate*, Vol. II, p. 285 *et seq.*

GARRISON, LLOYD K., "Government and Labor: The Latest Phase," *Columbia Law Review*, XXXVII, No. 6.

BELLOC, HILAIRE, *The Battleground: Syria and Palestine*, pp. 129–131.